For President and Mrs. Sills –
affectionately,
Holding
Feb. 3, 1948

Southern
Legacy

Hodding Carter

Hodding Carter

Southern Legacy

Louisiana State University Press
Baton Rouge

Contents

I.

The Broadsword Virtues

THIS IS WHAT Stephen Vincent Benét wrote near
the singing close of *John Brown's Body*, the truest
American epic poem:

> . . . Bury the bygone South
> Bury the minstrel with the honey-mouth
> Bury the broadsword virtues of the clan, . . .

But the broadsword virtues have not been buried,
nor, unless I misinterpret them, should they be. Call
them feudal or provincial or patriarchal or archaic.
They may be all these, but they represent also something deeper and longer lasting and more inspiriting;
a unity that fuses families and clans and, spreading
out, brings together whole peoples, marking them
with a certain likeness of manners and convictions and
purpose.

No Southerner should assert, in his pride, that we
have a patent on the virtue—or vice—of clan unity. It
can be discovered even today in such thinning New
England townships as have not been submerged by
multiplied new waves of settlers. It persists in the
rural and small-town Midwest, though with some-

1

what the same qualification. But no other section has, to such a degree as does the South, the unity of deep-rooted homogeneity, nor does this unity find elsewhere so uniform an outward expression.

Its less attractive expressions have been thoroughly publicized by a multitude of novelists, sociologists, pamphleteers, and unfriendly politicians. Our curiosity about the newcomer is sometimes more vindictive than neighborly, and the nonconformist among us feels soon the lash of censure. We still entertain harsh suspicions of the dissimilar, we are hounded by resentment of what the outsider proposes to do to and with us, and our easy anger is directed less at our own shortcomings than at those who would legislate or conduct loud missions against them. These faults we have in greater measure than do others elsewhere, and these others do not let us forget them.

But I believe that the broadsword virtues go deeper than the broadsword's unfriendly edge and that our unity is in its soul a wholesome thing. And because these virtues are simpler to describe than to define, I want to tell of them by telling something of the town in which I live, Greenville, which lies close by the Mississippi River, and a little of what I have seen and experienced there and elsewhere in the South.

In its strenuous past and its hopeful present Greenville is the South in microcosm, though it does not share the more ancient heritage of the southeastern seaboard. Only a little more than a century ago the

2

sites of Greenville and our surrounding small towns and plantations were soggy, cypress swamps, hidden from the sun. Here was and is the frontier South.

The people who came to this swampland and cleared and drained and planted it were mostly of a kind—which is not to say that men of other ancestries could not have done as well. But these white men bore mostly English and Scotch-Irish names, with a scattering of German and south-Irish stock. Few were immigrants or the sons of immigrants, and most of them had left behind in the seaboard states or in Kentucky or Tennessee generally similar conditions of life. They were principally farmers who called themselves planters, with a sprinkling of merchants and military and professional men.

When they reached the Mississippi, they settled first where the land had been built up from the swamps by silt deposits from centuries of the river's overflow. They brought some slaves with them, and as they prospered they bought others. And for a hundred and more years now, they and their descendants have clung to the river. The Mississippi was not always kind to them. They had to cope with the river in flood, which was a thing they could understand, and with yellow fever, which they could not understand, and which four times within a century decimated our town. During the Civil War, old Greenville was burned to the ground by a landing party from Federal gunboats because its elderly men and young boys who were not off to the war persisted in sniping at Porter's blue-jackets from the river's bank. Sometimes the planters made money from their cotton, but more often they did not; and they came to judge themselves and the later comers principally by their conduct in time of flood and war and epidemic and economic disaster, and not by their financial stability.

So these people who were much like each other at the beginning became even more alike. They suffered together the assault of yellow jack and the destructiveness of the spring inundation. They learned beside their charred homes to hate the forcible intruder and to suspect those shoddy scavengers who followed in victory. They met poverty together, and together they enjoyed the intermittent periods of grace, not foresightedly, but with the gusto and disregard for future leanness that even today accompany a good cotton year. Despite their own differences, despite the inevitable cowards and fools and knaves among them, their likenesses shaped them, and the broadsword virtues were cultivated however unconsciously. And out of it came the unity so baffling to the nonparticipant.

All that this unity brought forth is not good. But it is there, and I believe that the good outweighs the bad. Neighborliness and kindliness course deep where disaster has been shared; the hospitality of the frontier and the farm is the most unaffected and genuine of all; and the hand is opened most readily for giving by those who have known the hand's old emptiness.

But these are generalities and I can hear the sophis-

4

ticate laughing at them. So I will turn to the thirteen years for which this little Mississippi River city has been my home.

William Alexander Percy, who is dead now, made it possible for us to come to Greenville to start a competing newspaper after the urbane Greenvillian David L. Cohn had suggested it. Most people who know anything about the South know who Will Percy was, even if they have not read *Lanterns on the Levee,* the sad, lyric autobiography of a man who belonged rightly to an earlier century. In that flat land called the Delta, which lies between the Yazoo and the Mississippi, four generations of Percys had lived as leaders— almost as clan leaders, for the Deltans are a stubborn clan within a clan—not degenerating like William Faulkner's Sartorises but holding to what they had and confident in their strength and consciences and pride. With Will's father, whom the ignoble Vardaman defeated and succeeded in the United States Senate, their state-wide influence died; and Will, a sensitive mystic, had virtually confined himself to his garden and the interests of his community years before we came to Greenville. But he wanted an aggressive paper there, and he enlisted the financial support of others, so that our own capital was better than matched and we were able to produce a new daily newspaper in the worst of the depression years.

Even before we had taken over the established newspaper, and despite the frictions and partisanship of a competitive newspaper struggle in a small city, we were met with extraordinary friendliness and support. I would like to think that this reception was because of ourselves, but it was not. Here was the clan unity in action. We had come to Greenville because Will Percy believed in us, and he had persuaded others likewise to believe. That was enough for most of Greenville long before anyone could make any firsthand estimates. It was almost as if the Deltans were saying: "If Will Percy, Frank England, Joe Virden, Billy Wynn, Edmund Taylor, Dave Cohn, and Q. Strange think they're all right, that's good enough." Of course, because there are diverse factions within the Delta clan and because we made enemies by the kind of newspaper we published, we found ready opponents too. But the opposition could not call us outsiders, that most destructive of Southern labels, for we belonged by adoption even before we had published a first issue. There were no political implications to this identification. Our original stockholders—none of whom now have any holdings in the newspaper— differed among themselves on many local and regional and state issues; yet never did one of them try to impose a conviction or even influence an editorial decision.

But the Lord would have been hard put to help us if we had come as outsiders to start a new newspaper in Greenville. Another kind of business, yes. But not one in which the community has a proprietary concern.

Even in the two grimly competitive years before

6

we acquired the other newspaper, our critics were outwardly kind and friendly. It may be that the Southerner will generally be polite until he is angry enough with you to kill you. I discovered that while an uncomfortably large number of these new fellow townsmen were damning the "radical yellow sheet" among themselves, they were speaking favorably of it to visitors—and, of more immediate importance, they were subscribing.

But even immediate business success in a small city is a drear accomplishment if the newcomer is excluded from communal life. I am not making unflattering comparisons, but I know that in some parts of the United States the newly arrived must often wait a long time for a friendly gesture—perhaps because people elsewhere are more preoccupied with getting ahead than are the run of Southerners and therefore avoid unprofitable distractions. In our first few months in Greenville—and we were still in our quite immature twenties—we were entertained in at least a hundred homes, by elderly relics of long-departed gentry, by the desk sergeant at police headquarters, by our own bourbon-and-water-drinking contemporaries, by reminiscent couples who recalled that some distant cousin had married my wife's father's sister-in-law on his younger brother's side, by our stockholders, by hosts who resented the new paper because it was a threat to their friends who owned the old one, by hosts who hoped we played bridge and others who were glad we did not—and all of them giving us, as fellow clansmen, a genuine welcome to the most select community in the most advantageous county in the most lovable state ("with all its faults") in the most blessed section ("if only they understood us") in the world. I would not trade that welcome to Greenville for any experience we have ever had; and now that we are settled citizenry ourselves, we know that this overwhelming courtesy to the friends of friends is really just a way of telling our own friends that we like them.

In these diverse homes there was a curious and significant similarity of conversational topics. It seemed then—and I am positive of it now—that our hosts were dividing their fellow citizens into meaningful categories for our especial guidance. They told us about the "rabbit people," a name for the timid men who had fled in 1927 when the river overran the levees for the last time and swirled man-high through Greenville for six weeks. They chatted in mocking detail of other citizens whose conduct in time of more personal crisis had been considerably less than courageous. They did not group their fellow townsmen in categories of wealth and poverty, success and failure, erudition and ignorance, but by the way that men and women measure up to more forthright standards. I have wondered whether these new friends were not indirectly warning us that if we too did not measure up, the new paper would not last any longer than had the levees in 1927.

That does not make sense to a lot of people. A wise

man shuns trouble, plays it safe, thinks of the future, waits for the draft, gets occupational exemption, and realizes that while sticks and stones may break his bones words can never hurt him. But not the broadsword clansmen of the rural South, whom Stephen Vincent Benét called pistol-hearted, and who believe yet in his "scone on the hob for the sons of grief, but a knife in the ribs for the pleasant thief."

There are warmer expressions of this unity. A few months after we came to Greenville, I underwent a severe operation. By that time the town was taking sides openly in the fight between the two newspapers, only one of which could possibly survive. It happened that our nearest neighbors did not approve of our upstart publication; but when I was brought home from the hospital, I enjoyed throughout my convalescence a variety of delicacies prepared and sent over by these disapproving neighbors; and one of them even insisted on coming to sit in the house while my wife went to the newspaper office.

A year and a half later we had won our newspaper fight. In the very month of triumph my wife became perilously ill. Early one morning emergency blood transfusions were needed. There were close friends enough to give all the blood that was required, but through the lightning grapevine of the small city, scores of others learned within an hour or less of the emergency, and they came in the early dawn to the hospital or jammed the telephone lines, their anxious wish to help evident in their sleep-filled voices and eyes. And among the volunteers was a member of the family whose newspaper we had just taken over.

Not long afterward there occurred one of those tragi-comic events which make small-city newspaper publishing somewhat more exciting than our metropolitan brethren suppose. Angered by an editorial which he interpreted as a personal insult, a citizen telephoned that he was coming over to kill me. We are friends now, so let it suffice to say that although each of us had every intention of doing in the other, intervening circumstances fortunate for both of us kept him from my front porch where I was waiting shakily with shotgun and pistol.

But the rumor of impending gunplay circulated almost as fast as it would have taken him to walk from his home to mine. And so my vigil of several hours was continuously interrupted by telephone calls and personal visits. One officer of the law warned me that I should not fire until my adversary crossed the sidewalk. That would be trespass, he explained, and I would be held blameless for shooting him. The rumor grew during the Sabbath morning until it was said that I was to be attacked not by one irate man but by a veritable posse of friends whom he was leading.

Will Percy's adherents in particular began offering their services at this juncture, one of the most lovable among them reminding me that although he was getting old he was still the best shot in Mississippi— which he was. Many times since I have thanked God that the incident ended without injury or discredit to either of us; but had I called upon the police for protection that day, I might as well have closed shop.

As it was, the affair ended on a comical note a few nights later at the Country Club New Year's Eve dance. During a Paul Jones, in which partners separate at intervals to dance with whoever is nearest at the time, my wife found that her new partner was my late enemy. So they waltzed around while revelers sitting on the sidelines cocked their fingers in imitation of a pistol and happily chanted "bang-bang-bang."

Perhaps these personal stories illustrate only that we were accepted into the clan and do not indicate how this unity is expressed in a wider communal sense. And it can be argued that this clannishness means one thing for those who are admitted and another for those who are not. But I believe that this condition of Southern life makes also for a strong and generally beneficial civic cohesion.

In the fall of 1947 our small Jewish community was given a difficult quota in the first nation-wide United Jewish Appeal campaign. Incidentally, in no other region of the United States have the Jews become so integrated with the general population or have been less subject to discriminations than in the South, which is a warm and hopeful story in itself. Anyway, a few Protestant and Catholic citizens were invited to the somber dinner with which the Jewish community opened the local campaign. We saw a stark, shameful motion picture of the Jewish Gethsemane in Europe; and then a young Jewish war veteran from St. Louis told with heartbreaking anger of what he had seen at Dachau. It was not a happy occasion for anyone, this restatement in a Mississippi town of man's inhumanity, this shocking reminder to the Christians present that the mass crime of genocide is the ultimate result of religious and racial aversions.

At the end of the joyless program, the Jewish citizens began making individual pledges. Mal Robertshaw, a planter, a Catholic, and as compassionate a man as I have ever known, whispered to me. "We've got to help our friends out." he said. Our friends, not our Jewish friends or those poor devils, but our friends. So he stood and told our friends that we would guarantee a minimum of $5,000 from the Protestants and Catholics of Greenville.

Instead of $5,000 we raised $10,000, with the newspaper as the central collection medium. Mal Robertshaw, who was neither young nor well, went from business house to business house, and from friend to friend, turning in his collections each evening. Scores of checks from $2 to $1,000 came through the mails. The Catholic priest brought in his own donation and among the contributors were a Negro doctor and a Negro bootblack. What I like to remember is not the amount of the individual gifts but the number who gave.

Not long afterward the newspaper and the Protestant Ministerial Association jointly sponsored a collec-

12

tion of food, clothing, and usable farm implements which was to be loaded on a river barge—we named it the Friendship Barge—for eventual distribution in war-stricken areas. The central distributing agency was the Church World Service, an interdenominational Protestant organization. The first donation, an astounding fifty overcoats, came from the merchant who had been chairman of the United Jewish Appeal campaign; and it was the donations of clothing and shoes from our predominantly Jewish retail clothiers that ensured the successful dispatch of the Friendship Barge.

And now, as I write this story, a happy cycle of interfaith friendship and communal interdependence is being completed. Our Roman Catholics are also a minority group, though a considerably larger one than the Jewish community. For many years they have maintained a parochial school for white children and another for Negro children, both of them open to students of all faiths. These two schools carry one fifth of our entire school load, and like the public schools in our growing town, they are greatly overcrowded and inadequately equipped. Some time ago the Catholics determined to build a new school at a cost of $250,000, and by the summer of 1948 had raised among themselves about two thirds of that amount.

Word got around that they were finding the going difficult. So at summer's end, a group of non-Catholics met at Father Moloney's home for dinner. In the group were Methodists, Episcopalians, Presbyterians, Bap-

13

tists, and Jews. We went over the building estimates with Father Moloney and the Catholic layman who is directing the building campaign and offered to raise money for the new school. The Protestant-Jewish drive in behalf of a Catholic parochial school was undertaken, and the important fact was not that we raised the self-determined minimum of $20,000 but that we participated.

What these stories mean to me is that our unity is deeper and stronger than prejudices and that our homogeneity transcends conflicting beliefs and interests. This is the great virtue of the clan whose shortcomings are more perceptible.

There are other characteristics. The broadsword folk may be too respectful toward their patriarchs, especially in political matters. At one and the same time, they can be friendly and suspicious, close-minded and openhanded, tender and violent, self-assured and self-doubting. They live in what is relatively an outdoor, agricultural society, which is the society least susceptible to change, even change for the better. But I suggest that they have also escaped some social blights as well. They do not support as many psycho-analysts, write as many suicide notes, seek as many divorces, or indulge as zealously in what is called trifling as do the more cosmopolitan folk elsewhere—though I suspect that the last-named distinction does not stem from greater moral scruples but from the popularity of the unwritten law among Southern juries and spouses.

14

And the nearness to fields and forests and rivers has an identifying quality of its own. In the winter of 1948 I began hunting again after years of thinking I was too busy to take time out. A frequent hunting companion was a game warden whom I had hitherto known but casually, and who is altogether frank in his opinions and appraisals. One murky afternoon while we squatted in a corn and bean field waiting for the doves to come in, he told me that a number of his friends did not have much use for me or my ideas. He added that he did not agree with me always either.

"But there's one thing sure," he said, his eyes searching the gray sky. "There can't be too much wrong with a fellow who likes to hunt."

He does not know it, but right then and there I became a confirmed hunter. If you are going to live among the broadsword folk, you can carry nonconformity just so far.

2.

Grandmother Was Emphatic

WHEN I WAS a brash youngster of seventeen, with a year in a Yankee college behind me, I visited my maternal grandmother in Concordia Parish, Louisiana, across the river from Natchez.

She was a dainty little lady, given to delicate scents and a hairdo that displayed her white curls to advantage; but her femininity was no more pronounced than was her domination over the conglomeration of daughters, nephews, nieces, and grandchildren who surrounded her as permanent guests or occasional visitors.

There were eighteen of us thus gathered together at midday dinner on a summer day of my visit back in 1924. Grandmother presided at the head of the table. I sat midway at her left and, in the hubbub of unrelated conversation, I was learnedly holding forth to a cousin on the evils of the resurgent Ku Klux Klan. I had just said that the Klan was a rotten, no-good, and un-American organization, or words to that effect, when I became conscious of frightened signals from my cousin and a sudden, awesome hush. I looked toward

16

the head of the table. Obviously grandmother was about to speak to us.

But grandmother's words were for no one but me. She had heard only my concluding comment on the Klan, and her failure to understand that it was not *the* Klan I was castigating, but only a spurious, latter-day imitation thereof, was my undoing.

"Stand up, young man," she said. She had a flair for the dramatic. I stood up.

"Your year up North seems to have disagreed with you," she began. "Did they teach you to say what you have just said about the Ku Klux Klan?"

It was too late to rectify her error or mine. For a long five minutes grandmother retold the warm, familiar story. With her own hands she had made my grandfather's Klan robes. Practically singlehanded, though with some minor assistance from a legendary Captain Norwood—"the second most handsome man in the Confederate Army"—grandfather had saved a large section of the South through some well-timed night riding and an unerring aim. Had it not been for grandfather and a few lesser giants in the land, no man's life and no white woman's virtue would have been safe. I had heard the story since childhood, loved it, believed it, believe some part of it even today. But I had gone back on my raising. I had denounced the Klan. I was a traitor to the South, thanks to my parents' grave mistake in permitting me to go to college in Maine.

I tried once, but only once, to interrupt with an explanation. My cousins were giggling. One or two aunts

17

were nodding ready approval of grandmother's fury. I was hopelessly lost.

"Leave the table, young man," grandmother concluded. "You may apologize to me when we have finished dinner."

Later, of course, I received a qualified pardon after grandmother finally came to understand that I meant no sacrilege. But thereafter, in her presence, I kept my thoughts on the Klan, past, present, or future, to myself.

I have told this story many times since that uncomfortable dinner hour, as an amusing anecdote of my youth. I did not understand its implications for a long time, nor, I suspect, did many who heard the tale. For it seemed to be simply one of those incomprehensible Southern incidents, having no reference to things as they are and altogether out of place in the world today.

But this interpretation is wrong.

I was born forty-two years ago, just midway between the close of the War Between the States and the present. Similarly located in meaningful time are hundreds of thousands, even millions, of white Southerners of my age and older, who represent the thinking, the political directions, the economic attitudes of our badgered South. Almost every one of us, farmer, city man, mountaineer, teacher, preacher, poor white or so-called "Bourbon," was close to some fabulous father or grandfather, some remembering grandmother, to whom, in our childhood and even our young manhood, the war and its aftermath was a personal, bitter, and sacred reality. And if, in their declining years, they embroidered fact with fancy, our inheritance was no less real, our conviction of wrongful treatment no less strong, our resultant idealization no less significant.

For, in folk history, the eighty-four years since Appomattox is a short span, especially for people who were on the losing side. I remember bicycling through Ireland once, in the mid-twenties, and stopping for a cup of water at a peasant's hut. Rebellion was unusually rife in Ireland then, and the old woman with whom I chatted had nothing good to say for the English. Just four miles up the road, she told me, the English had tied 200 God-fearing Irishmen to stakes and burned them. I was incredulous, for I had not come across this grim tale in any reports of the Black and Tan or rebel excesses.

"My God," I exclaimed, "when did they do that?"

"It was Cromwell," she said. "The dir-r-ty dog."

The South is scarcely less persevering in remembering its dirty dogs, in bedaubing some who were not dirty, and in discrediting what might be offered as the other side of the story. Did we not have our grandfathers and grandmothers as proof? Do we not remember the old men from the Confederate home, men still hale in 1916, whose rebel yells turned the first showings of *The Birth of a Nation* into emotional pandemonium and who assured the children of nine and ten that life had been just like that, only worse? It was as

19

true as gospel itself that Ben Butler had stolen spoons and ordered his troops to despoil the women at New Orleans; that Sherman was Satan incarnate who laughed at his bummers' toll of starving women and children along his line of march, and that Thaddeus Stevens took a Negro wife, and sought to provide white Southern wives for his Negro cohorts.

Profane history has not triumphed over such articles of faith. And, as a corollary, some of the bittersweet morsels which fed our minds have not themselves been made more savory by actual history. While in school in the East, I met and liked a student of considerable means. His grandfather, who shall be nameless here, actually gave the family fortune its sizable start by dishonest trafficking in federally seized cotton. About the time this Eastern fortune was being accumulated in the immediate wake of the war, my great-grandmother, whose husband had been mortally wounded at Shiloh, journeyed to Washington to seek a presidential pardon for herself so that she could regain her modest properties in New Orleans. We have that pardon, signed by Andrew Johnson. In it the engraved descriptive phrase, "the late traitor," was amended in ink, with the word "traitress" scrawled above the scratched-out "traitor," and her name following thereafter. And speaking of contraband-cotton fortunes, my mother's family dreamed for years of the windfall that would come our way when Congress approved the Southern cotton claims. Only Congress never did.

These unseparated truths and fantasies did strange things to those of us who stand midway in the eighty-four-year time span. They explained inertia and genteel poverty too well. My Ku Klux grandfather, I was convinced, would have left unnumbered acres to his widow had it not been for war and Reconstruction; and I still remember my shocked disbelief when my wryly humorous mother once suggested that another reason was his postwar inability to fill inside straights when the chips represented cotton land. They provided a background which gave approval to a childish game of draping ourselves in white sheets and chasing Negro children through the woods with guns. They gave sanctity to the pronouncements of our Episcopal rector's son, who would argue with the high-school history teacher and declare baldly that Abraham Lincoln was an atheist and the illegitimate brother of Jefferson Davis, and that slavery was the foreordained and natural state of Africans.

Every now and then since those earlier days, I remind myself hopefully that, after all, these determining factors were waning even in my childhood. My own three sons would not be thus conditioned by any past. We would see to it, my wife and I, that their pride in the South and its past would be balanced, as they grew up, with proper emphasis upon the new South and the nation of which it is an irrevocable and generally wholesome part. None of that ancestor-worship business for them, no sir. And this shaping would be easy, because they had lived away from the South for almost five years during the recent war: the oldest from his sixth to his eleventh year, the second from his first year to his sixth. Even the baby, born in Washington, had been almost a Northerner for a year.

I am not so sure about that now. In June, 1946, after only a year of being home in Mississippi, we started out for our annual summer in Maine. The first night's stop was at Chattanooga, and that meant a trip to the top of Lookout Mountain and considerable, if improvised, emphasis upon a long-ago battle among the clouds. The end of the second day brought us to Lexington, Virginia. We left Lee Chapel at Washington and Lee University, laden with Confederate flags, our minds past-haunted with the words of the soft-spoken curator, whose first assumption that we were "non-Southern" I had corrected hastily and almost indignantly. Later in the morning, the older boys became starry-eyed and silent at VMI before the proud canvas that depicted the charge of the boy cadets of VMI at New Market; and we left Lexington with the Stars and Bars waving wildly from the windows of the car. In the late afternoon of that day we reached Gettysburg, and that was our undoing. First, we visited the sad, majestic battlefield, and then the ghost-ridden museum, in whose amphitheater one can look down upon an electrically controlled topographical map of Gettysburg, where changing battalions of red and blue lights illustrate the lecturer's account of the bloody campaign. When the lecturer finished, the two older boys were disconsolate.

"That was a tough one for us to lose," Hodding III said moodily. "Anyhow, we killed more of them than they did of us, didn't we?"

I roused myself from inwardly cursing at Longstreet and wondering where in hell Stuart could have been all that time, to remind him that it all happened for the best, and, anyway, where would we be today if we weren't a united country?

So there it is, this persistent initial legacy. Play "America" or the "Star Spangled Banner" before a Southern audience, and it will stand at required attention. Play "Dixie" and you had better stick cotton in your ears.

Let alone, the spirit of which these stories are symbols is harmless enough; a little pathetic perhaps, and naïve and provincial. Let alone, it will, of course, wear itself out someday. Not tomorrow or next year or the next. But someday. But it is not let alone by those least worthy to capitalize upon it, the politicians who subvert the Southern legacies to confuse their constituents and perpetuate themselves, though it can be said honestly that such instruments are losing their effectiveness.

Meanwhile, let us see this stubborn legacy for what it is. A defensive thing which stiffens the spine of the colonially exploited and prideful and poor against the urban and sophisticated and economically entrenched.

23

A rallying point for conservatism against the impact of change and of ideas. A shared past, drawing together a long-related folk against the newcomer and the alien. A shield against the constant thrusting from the outside. And a tragically employed excuse for wrongs since committed and right things left undone.

This emotional heritage is difficult of understanding for the detached, present-minded, and amiable non-Southerners to whom that war of our grandfathers is a struggle happily over, properly won by the side which should have won, and now properly relegated to the limbo of the past. It is even more difficult of understanding for those new, zealous historians who take as a starting point the assumption that the South deserved whatever it got; that, in fact, its Bourbons came off too lightly; and that the war and Reconstruction were essentially a struggle between the submerged classes—black and white in the South lumped carefully together—on the one side, and on the other, the spirit of reaction so oversimply represented by a diabolical figure, the ante- and post-bellum Southern Planter.

Nevertheless, the stories told by aging men and women to young boys persist, and there is more than legend to them. What my grandmother remembered in microcosm represented a macrocosm of disaster whose material and spiritual effects are as readily recognizable to the psychologist as to the historian. The South's wealth was as completely gone at the close of the Civil War as is that of any postwar European

24

country today, and there was no Marshall Plan. Its banks were closed, its currency without value, its bonds and insurance worthless too. Its principal single item of wealth, two billion dollars' worth of slaves, was destroyed. The South's largest cities were ravaged by bombardment and fire, many of its smaller towns were desolated, and the scorched-earth technique had left its countryside, where the Union armies had passed, a desert. Two thirds of its railroads were in ruins. Land dropped in value from $50.00 to as low as $3.00 an acre and was sold for taxes, and at the close of 1865 an estimated 500,000 people in three states alone existed at starvation levels. Returning Confederates, with no clothing other than their ragged uniforms, were forced to remove the military buttons—or have them forcibly removed by Negro troops. Those among them who had been veterans of earlier American wars were stricken from the pension lists. Though courts still functioned, military commissions tried defendants in cases far removed from their ordinary jurisdiction, and the longest military occupation in modern history was accompanied by a political vengefulness that healed no wounds.

These things, however vaguely identified, were in my grandmother's mind as she lectured me there at the dinner table. Secondhand, they have persisted in the memory of many others and they cannot be shrugged off.

And I am thereby reminded of another story which, better than any other I have heard, illustrates this

Southern legacy of resentment over the outcome of an ancient war. The story's heroine is in her eighties, the daughter of one of Stonewall Jackson's bodyguard, and indomitably Virginian. Not so many years ago, at an age when few of us would be interested in further pursuit of learning, she enrolled in a university summer course in the history of the South. One day during the session, the lecturer made the usual comment, namely, that it was best that the war had ended with a Northern victory. Later on during his talk he made the same apologetic interjection. The smoldering little lady could stand his treason no longer. She rose from her chair and interrupted him.

"Professor," she challenged, "you keep saying that it was best that the North won the war. But how do you know? We didn't get a chance to even *try* it our way."

3.

Faith of Our Fathers

THE SOUTH MAY BE described as the Bible belt in the same offhand and derisive way that the Eastern seaboard can be identified as the barbiturate belt, the roaring, raw cities of the Midwest the tommy-gun belt, and the West Coast the divorce belt.

But the religious identification goes deeper. Though the citadels crumble, the South remains the great western-world stronghold of Protestant, fundamentalist Christianity. As such it is the legatee of the spiritually zestful, mystic, and masochistic soul of its largely Celtic forebears.

In Tennessee, devout folk still sing praises to the hero of their brush with monkey-minded sons of darkness:

William Jennings Bryan is dead, he died one Sabbath
    day.
So sweetly was the king asleep, his spirit passed away;
He was at Dayton, Tennessee, defending our dear
    Lord,
And as soon as his work on earth was done, he went to
    his reward.

27

He fought the evolutionists, the infidels and fools
Who are trying to ruin the minds of our children in
the schools,
By teaching we came from monkeys and other things
absurd
By denying the works of our blessed Lord and God's
own holy word.

In Mississippi, Tennessee, and Arkansas, the teaching of evolutionary theories is still technically illegal; and, in the spring of 1948, the University of Arkansas turned down a proposed course which listed the first chapter of Genesis under "Myths of Creation." The camp meeting, brought up to date with loud-speakers and cooling systems, can, in rural Southern localities, outdraw Betty Grable and break even with Jim Folsom, Herman Talmadge, and John Rankin. The political pressures, in certain material directions, of the Baptist and Methodist churches, and to some extent the Presbyterian, are powerful and not uniformly misapplied. New churches continue to be built, though it is somewhat more difficult now to fill the pulpits than the pews. There is in the South an unexhausted reservoir of simple piety, which, if directed toward true acceptance of the Sermon on the Mount and the Christian concept of man's brotherhood, could and may yet effect a more profound change in regional social-racial patterns than any legislation devised toward that end.

Few Southerners find it easy to look upon these facts with detachment. That thing called the old-

28

time religion is in the blood of most of us, and if it is laughed at, the laughter has as accompaniment an almost inescapable inner, esoteric warning that the ways of God are not to be mocked by man. A little over a century ago, the South of the Scotch-Irish farmer and frontiersman was swept by an evangelical flood that submerged the gentlemanly Jeffersonian skepticism and Anglican liberalism, leaving on the Southeastern seaboard alone an isolated high ground of doubt and investigation.

Through the back country rode the indomitable Methodist circuit riders. Rough-tongued men and women were propelled below the surface of rushing rivers and obscure streams by the sanctified hands of self-discovered Baptist preachers, and rose choking, to scream the glory of God and their temporary abnegation of red liquor, eye gouging, and painted Jezebels. This was the Second Awakening, primitive, democratic, and certain, and religious liberalism in the South died before its surge. Victim, too, but of secular and sectional considerations, was the early revivalist concern with the black man's freedom; the Protestant churches of the South became the inspired spokesmen for the institution of slavery, entrenching themselves the more solidly thereby, and Christianity, Northern version, a distorted, satanic misinterpretation of the gospel that doomed the sons of Ham. God had providentially placed the poor, heathen African in the charge of the South. God was on the South's side. It was as simple as that.

29

"The parties in this conflict are not merely abolitionists and slaveholders," proclaimed the Reverend
James Henley Thornwell, Presbyterian divine and
president of South Carolina College in 1850. "They
are atheists, socialists, communists, red republican
jacobins on the one side, and the friends of order and
regulated freedom on the other. In one word, the
world is the battleground, Christianity and atheism
the combatants; and the progress of humanity at
stake."

Organized religion in the South became the
mighty fortress of the *status quo;* the revival ex-
horters assumed the dignity and the defense of the
ruling classes, uncompromising as ever in their
castigation of the sins of the flesh but equally
adamant in their justification of man's ownership of
man. A Calvinistic God had ordained slavery; those
who rebelled against it were in rebellion against God.
Narrow fanaticism, strict and literal interpretation
of the Bible, defense of the established order and its
apostles, orthodoxy discernible even among the
anarchical multitude of sects—these were the South's
religious answer to the abolitionist, the hell-damned
skeptic, the new, restless scientist, and the worldly
outsider.

And that, to a lessening and challenged degree,
is the religious South's position today.

Yet, it is unfair to so limit the impact of Protestant-
ism upon the South. God was an anthropomorphic He-
braic avenger, with terrible lightning in his eyes, but

the Christ child was gentle and forgiving, loving man, loving even the least of these, even the retarded black, God-ordained to be a hewer of wood and drawer of water. A tribal God punished the wrongdoer, but it was the tender Christ who illumined the path of righteousness, who waited beside the still waters, who whispered in the ear of the tempted, who cried out in agony, "Father, forgive them; for they know not what they do."

I know both sides. My family was Presbyterian, not as rigid as the parents of my Baptist and Methodist playmates, for whom dancing and cardplaying were sins only surreptitiously indulged in, but rigid enough and to spare. Sunday school, church, Young People's League, prayer meeting. On Sunday, no funny papers, no movies, no ball games, no profane music. Family prayers every night during a prolific family's summer reunions, with a gay, emancipated aunt at the piano, making ragtime of the gospel hymns, while a horde of cousins, deliciously afraid that God might strike her dead for her rhythmic sacrilege, filled the seashore night with "Shall We Gather at the River," "Beulah Land," and "Stand Up, Stand Up for Jesus." We *knew* God was everywhere. The children's catechism said so. We knew, too, that a still small voice would report to us, and to God, of wrongdoing. And, best of all, we knew that the little Lord Jesus would get us out of trouble if we asked forgiveness. I have never heard a more beauti-

31

ful phrase than my paternal grandmother's metaphor for the air itself. "God's breath," she said, "it is God's breath." I know, too, that none of us were untouched by the beauty of her faith, by her sureness as to good and evil, in the formative years when consciences grow or wither.

And now the other side. When I was fifteen and yet undisturbed by doubting, a revivalist came to town. Those were the days of Gypsy Smith, for whom I once proudly passed and shamefully dropped a collection plate, and Billy Sunday and lesser but just as loud fighters for the Lord. This exhorter was in the category of the lesser, but he had a way with him, and within two days the news of his success with the town's sinners packed the chilly church for matinee and evening performances. Near the end of his week's visitation, when almost all except the most casehardened had been saved, I went to a night meeting with two friends, partly out of curiosity as to how people performed publicly when they were saved, but certainly without any agnostic doubting of the message the revivalist would bring that night. The Bible was still the unchallenged word.

Our small, diffident group sat in the back of the church, around the wood stove, bunched nervously together while the revivalist worked himself and his audience to a numbing hysteria of devotion. We sang the hymns lustily enough, and at first I was awed by the man's intensity and his audience's response. Men and women, and even children whom I had never suspected of being damned, began hitting the glory trail, crowding to the foot of the pulpit, some crying and one woman gagging with nausea. I became conscious of a strange, sickening resentment, a disbelief that this performance had any basic relationship to religion. It was my first such feeling and it made me want to leave. I wish I had. But we stayed by the stove, watching the hypnotized converts move forward, until, at last, there were no more volunteers. Then the revivalist moved upon the rest of the worshipers, most of whom had undoubtedly been publicly saved on previous nights. He called upon everyone who knew himself to be a sinner to stand and acknowledge his salvation through the blood of the Lamb. As men and women and children began rising from their seats, the revivalist stepped down from the platform, walking up the aisles with arms upraised, to urge the slow or reluctant to get up or be forever lost. The members of our small group looked at each other. Something went cold inside me, and I shook my head negatively to the others. I had decided I was not going to get up, and that this shouting man could not doom me with his alternatives. In a few minutes, everyone in the church was standing except the three adolescent boys around the stove.

We had hoped to remain undetected, being far in the rear and removed from the pews, but he spotted us and in another moment towered over us like the angel at the gates of Eden. He exhorted us to stand. I kept my head down, not daring to look at him nor at the incredulous faces that turned to stare at us.

The revivalist rejoiced in the challenge. He entreated us in the name of the forgiving God and warned us of hell-fire to come. He called upon our parents—happily none of them were present—to intervene. He laid hands upon us, commanding us to acknowledge our sinfulness. One of my friends, frightened out of his wits by now—as I was—rose, leaving two young sinners to face the wrath of God. And we stuck it out to the horror of everyone present. I wanted to kill that man. I was afraid of mortal punishment and of my parents' reaction when they heard of this spectacle we were making. But we sat and sat, our faces burning, our ears ringing, our eyes downcast, and finally the revivalist gave up.

My parents, quickly advised of their son's strange behavior, were shocked but sympathetic. They did not like the notoriety. The best thing to do, they said, was to stay away from such meetings if I did not like them.

I have never attended a revival since. There are easier ways to break with fundamentalism and the God of wrath.

The vengeful tradition persists. Once, years later, I suggested editorially that a Holy Roller revival in our town remove itself beyond the city limits because the noise was disturbing to Christians and sinners alike. The participants were handling snakes

34

and white-hot coal-oil-lamp chimneys, getting the shakes and the shouts, and it was not pleasant. So, the next day it was noised around that I was to be denounced in the Unknown Tongue that night. I went to hear it. My Holy Roller friends made certain that their listeners would know who was being denounced. In the middle of the unintelligible jabber-jabber-jabber of the Unknown Tongue, they would occasionally shout my name or that of my newspaper.

Such performances mean religion yet to too many Southerners. Some powerful denominations in Mississippi still conduct state-wide days or hours of prayer whenever the legislature undertakes gingerly to repeal or modify our unavailing liquor laws; but I have not known them to concentrate similarly when forward social legislation is being considered. We have an eighteen-year-old printer's apprentice in my newspaper plant who, in the name of religion, refuses to go to a movie, play cards, dance, or drink even a Coca-Cola. And I know two Protestant ministers to whom inclusion of a rabbi in a ministerial alliance is repugnant because they hold the Jews eternally responsible for the death of Christ.

Tragedy lies in this mean dissipation of the tremendous Southern reservoir of faith. Fortunately, that tragedy is being increasingly perceived by churchmen and laymen, particularly the younger men and women, and from their awareness comes not only future hope but present action. In seeming contradiction to the constant evidence of misdirected zeal, many churches of the South—Protestant and Catholic alike—are far ahead of their memberships in the areas of social action, which is as it should be and must be. It is not uncommon today for ministers to espouse constitutional rights for Negroes or to bespeak applied Christianity in economic relationships. Some of them pay for their daring. There is much muttering in the South against radical tendencies in the churches, the Federal Council of the Churches of Christ and the YMCA and the YWCA being especial targets, and the spirit of schism is strong. But by the very fact that the minister is still a man apart, ordained by God, his courage and vision can command respect if not emulation. As an example, I can cite the experience of a devoted young clergyman, who less than a year after he came to our town preached a blunt, biting sermon on racial discrimination. He was violently criticized, some members left his congregation, and it was predicted that he would not last a month longer. He is still here and I know that he has won converts.

And where could be found more fertile fields for crusading than the churches of the essentially rural South? There the communal stream runs strong. There, as much as human frailties and human concerns permit, men and women dwell for a short time beyond themselves, seeking refreshment of the spirit, warming themselves in the bright sunlight of the churchyard beneath a brighter if uncomprehended sun. There, fleetingly, they are malleable to good;

36

there the inheritance of ardent faith could pry open the hearts to the words of the preacher who finds his text in Galatians:

"There is neither Jew nor Greek, there is neither bond nor free, there is neither male nor female: for ye are all one in Christ Jesus."

4.

Like a Member of the Family

WHENEVER I HEAR a fellow Southerner exaggerate sentimentally the old, fading comradeship between Negro boy and white, or a militant critic deny or decry that such relationship ever truly existed, I think of Son McKnight.

Son and I never visualized ourselves at the time as representing a maudlin expression of responsibility of one race for another or, on the other hand, as being symptomatic of an unutterably feudal and one-sided caste system. I am sure he did not think of himself as a "white man's nigger," nor was I conscious of wearing shining armor because we were friends.

Son and I were not rarities thirty years ago. We would be uncommon if we shared a boyhood today.

Son was the third of six children and about nine years old, as was I, when his widowed mother attached her hungry family to our own. Her husband had been shot to death, quite unnecessarily, by a quick-triggered deputy who succeeded in killing or maiming a number of men, white and Negro, before his own unmourned demise. The father had died in his own front yard, before the eyes of his hysterical wife and children, crying for water which Son says the deputy forbade.

Anyway, his aunt, who was our cook, told my mother about them, and in a short while we had to all purposes adopted the children. The oldest girl became a maid of sorts, the second girl a generally useless supernumerary, and Son my own charge and delight, whose duties were limited at first to giving the lawn an occasional lick and promise with the mower.

From that time until I entered college, Son was companion, body servant and bodyguard. I know it is no longer proper to dwell fondly on such a relationship, but I cannot help it. Son was sparring partner when my younger brother and I first put on boxing gloves, pulling his own punches because he was tougher and harder than we, and laughing at our ineffective swinging. He was the catcher when we tried to learn to pitch curves. Once I was whipped by my father because, after the circus came to town, I stood Son up against the back wall of the garage as a target and practiced knife throwing with an assortment of pocket and kitchen cutlery. On another occasion I saved him from a sure whipping. My mother's car had run out of gas a few blocks from home, when Son and I were on the back seat. Mother walked home, after waiting impatiently for us to return from a near-by garage with an emergency gallon of gasoline. Son, who was then about eleven, told me he knew how to drive well enough to get the car home; and so he did, managing things very well until he reached the porte-cochere. Before he could stop the car he had sadly damaged one pillar, one automobile, and a grapevine trellis that connected the porte-cochere with the garage. I hid him in our army tent in the back yard while my father hunted for him, finally begging him off by saying that it was my idea. On that day was born our great—and never realized—plan for him to be my chauffeur when we grew up.

Not all of our time together was so idly spent. He had never gone to school, nor did he ever; but for a couple of years I spent an hour or so in the kitchen after supper, three or four times a week, teaching Son a mighty little reading and writing and arithmetic. Later I became briefly a wage earner, at twelve, with a newspaper-delivery job that paid me a dollar a week. My mother insisted that I wear, even during business hours, a Buster Brown collar-and-short-socks outfit, which was definitely not *de rigueur* among the street-sale newspaper boys who also met the afternoon train that brought the papers from New Orleans. Thus clad, I went alone to the station the first day on the job and came home dishevelled and mauled. So I took Son along the next day. The two of us—mostly Son—got even with the little station gang, and he broke a thumb in his enthusiasm, though we did not find that out until the next day. That night, the town marshal came to the house and told my father that the parents of one of our opponents had demanded that he handle—a euphemism for whip—the Carter nigger for fighting white boys. My father asked me what happened, and after I told him he advised the marshal that there would not be any such punishment for Son and that he would continue to accompany me to the station. Small towns and my father being what they were, that was that.

After I went away to college, Son got a job in the box factory. We continued to see each other at Christmas holidays and during those summers when I came home, but there was a difference. I was Mister Hodding to him, and to me he was a nearly grown young Negro, earning good money and spending much of it—his aunt said disapprovingly—on whiskey. Nevertheless, convinced that in a few years the world would be mine, he would bring up, time and again, our ancient agreement that he was to be my chauffeur. Matters came to a head my senior year. Son had heard that I had a girl. He concluded erroneously that marriage was imminent and that I would soon be a man of family. He reminded me that he was expecting to be my chauffeur as soon as the event took place. I pointed out that a young married couple could hardly afford a car, much less a driver. Son studied the problem a moment and then came up with a solution that I will never forget.

"Look here, Hod—Mister Hodding," he suggested,

"I've got almost $200 saved up. I'll buy the car on time, and do the drivin' and we won't tell nobody." He meant it.

Then our paths separated. I went to work in New Orleans, and Son, back home, developed what they called a "wild streak." He had several losing brushes with the law as a result of such minor offenses as drunkenness and fighting, and my father told me that he was afraid Son was headed for trouble. He was. One day Son walked into the office of the United Press in New Orleans, where I was working, and told me that he had stabbed another colored man in Hammond. No, he had not killed him, but the police had tried to catch him so he had come to New Orleans, where one of his sisters was now living. He had to have (1) five dollars and (2) a letter from me that would get him a job, and I must not tell anyone he was here. A ready accessory after the fact, I gave him the money and the most fulsome letter in all the history of character certification, and he did get a job in a garage. But he grew tired of city life in a few months, and on one of his frequent visits to the UP office he asked me to find out if it was all right for him to go home now. I wrote Dad, and Dad inquired around. Son's adversary had recovered, and it was "just a Negro cutting scrape anyhow," so it was all right for Son to return. He told me good-by, and returned to Hammond to marry and, in a manner of speaking, settle down.

A couple of years later I also was making preparations to wed. Son, who kept a close check on me through my parents, turned up the next week end I was home, and told me to fix it so he could attend the wedding. That assignment presented a few difficulties. The wedding was to be a damnably formal home affair. Son could, of course, help pass the refreshments at the reception, but the double living room, the dining room, the long hall, and probably the clothes closets would be jammed with guests. I explained this to him. He said just to get him in and he could manage.

And manage he did, with the aid of probably a quart of bolstering punch, surreptitiously imbibed before the first strains of Lohengrin. The only face I distinctly remember at my wedding was Son's, some three feet above the multitude in the jammed hall. He had simply nudged his way, with profuse excuse-me's, to a fragile chair against the wall and, standing upon it, waved reassuringly to me at frequent intervals during the ceremony.

I was jobless a few months later, so my wife and I started our first newspaper, in Hammond, and soon thereafter were at home to our friends in a rambling old cottage, so old that its only heating came from open fireplaces in each room. On the first cold morning, a little after dawn, I was awakened by my wife's terrified scream. Just as frightened, I sat bolt upright, cursing myself for not having a pistol by the bed. A Negro man was in the room. But the man was Son, kneeling by the fireplace with paper and kindling and firewood. There were no snap locks on our doors, only the old-fashioned turn-key locks, and Son had a skeleton key.

Not long afterwards, he and I conspired to provide him with a house of his own. My father had a small, unimproved piece of property in the Negro section of Hammond, a weedy lot which he had forgotten about and of which I knew nothing. But somehow, Son knew the status of that lot. He turned up at our newspaper office one day and said that if I would stand good for $150 worth of lumber and such, he knew where he could build a house. He had accumulated some bricks, he said, and secondhand timbers, and all he needed was boards and roofing and wallpaper, and $150 would see him through. After some prodding he revealed the site on which he planned to build, pointing out that it was unlikely that Dad would ever drive by it, as the road was in a bad state of repair. So I went into the building business. Dad found out sooner than we had expected, because he noticed the next year that the small taxes were trebled, but there was not much he could do about it then. That little house, built by Son alone, has since been added to, painted, equipped with indoor plumbing, and furnished; and many a family would be glad to live in it today. When I was home for Thanksgiving a year ago, he invited me to see his latest improvement, a fifth room. In the little living room was a twenty-two-year-old picture of me as a

44

college junior, and beneath it were the copies of my books which I had dutifully sent him.

And recently, for a very short time, I joined Son in another enterprise. For the past ten years or more, he has worked in a dry-cleaning establishment as cleaner and presser, earning moderately good wages. Not so long ago he decided that he could do better if he were in business for himself. His minuscule savings could not swing the cost of the necessary minimum for secondhand equipment, so I found myself, by a not so singular coincidence, a distant, minor partner in a pressing-shop business that never quite materialized.

That brings the story up to date. If I have dwelt overlong on it, it is simply because I have found personal pleasure in setting down a tale that in its broad outline is familiar to many Southerners. All of it is true and I have no apologies for any of its aspects, only a warm delight in its thirty-year duration. To those who can and probably will riddle it with the obvious comments as to its imperfections, I can say only that there are many thousands of white and Negro men today who can similarly find at least this same common ground. Certainly the relationship was feudal and, I suppose, made no contribution to interracial advancement. The other side of the coin is that such friendships were, if nothing more, a buffer between the Son McKnights of the South and their positions in the disregarded mass; and, for the white participants, a voyage of discovery taken by too few of us and an unwitting means of denying the shibboleths. Son is better off, in more than a material way, for it, and so am I.

And yet, looking back, a disquieting realization intrudes. The Sons of my boyhood were almost always in the same pattern, lost little souls, uneducated, faithful, asking and expecting nothing more than the white folks' largesse, and ending up more often as discarded retainers than as pressing-shop proprietors. And for each of these relatively fortunate ones there must have been many others, their ambition not yet dulled at nine, dreaming of the chances that education would give and doomed to its denial.

The truth of it is that most of us were—as many among us still are—distrustful of the educated young Negro and the young Negro seeking education. They disturbed both the illusion and the reality of the interracial scene. It would not have occurred to my father, or to me in my boyhood, to help educate a Negro's son for teaching or medicine or the ministry or intelligent agriculture. We never thought of Son as being representative of that tenth man who has a contribution of his own to make. He was the individual, favored exception to the harsh rule.

Today the Sons have a somewhat better chance, even without the hand that once stretched out in limited comradeship. But relatively, the odds are long yet, and the individual hand is rarely there.

46

There lingers a reluctance in the South to transfer our assistance from the vanishing youngster whom we defined and recognized as a good nigger to another who must be as readily recognized and accepted as a good citizen.

But I would have as hard a time explaining this to many white Southerners as to Son himself.

5.

Not Much of a Man if He Hadn't

THE KILLING which led to my only service on
a jury had been commonplace.

An irascible, middle-aged Louisianian, whose
house adjoined a small-town filling station, had been
for some time the butt of the station attendants'
jokes. Despite his warnings that he had had enough
of their tomfoolery, and though aware of his short
temper, they nevertheless persisted in badgering him
until, one morning, he stood on his front porch and
fired a couple of loads of buckshot into them. One
man, an innocent customer, was killed. One of the
jesters was maimed for life and another was less
severely wounded.

The state brought charges only of manslaughter,
though there was evidence of premeditation. At the
trial, the defense and prosecution witnesses were in
general agreement as to the events leading up to the
shooting, and the shooting itself. The defense attorneys pleaded self-defense.

No one in the parish except the relatives of the
wounded men—the dead man was a stranger—was
particularly aroused by the slaying. Passion killings

48

were an old story. Twenty had been committed in the parish in the recent past, and this one became mildly notable only because it was one of four which had resulted in jury trials.

Neither the state nor the defense wasted many challenges. I was accepted for jury duty after duly swearing that I had no fixed opinions.

The trial lasted three days, and my service as a juror was pleasant enough. Nine of my fellow jurors were farmers. The others were townsmen; and, at twenty-six, I was younger than the rest by ten years or more. The farmers had fun with me after my wife brought me a suitcase containing such ridiculous luxuries as pajamas, books, and magazines. But we got along well together, enjoying the tremendous meals at the boardinghouse to which a deputy escorted us thrice daily, and whiling away the evenings in the sleeping quarters in the courthouse attic with heated political wrangles and more amiable discussions of hard times, crops, absent acquaintances, and women.

I was the most inexperienced, the youngest, and the brashest, and it may be that these qualifications led my fellows to elect me foreman. I took seriously the role of peer of a killer brought to judgment, the professional curiosity of a newspaperman heightened by my own participation in the trial. I was certain, after hearing the testimony, that the defendant was guilty. Unquestionably he had been goaded by two of his victims. But the owlish old fellow had answered gibes with buckshot, and to my way of thinking he was guilty of manslaughter.

On the afternoon of the third day, the jury retired to decide its verdict. I felt tense and a little sick, even though I knew that we would not have to debate whether to take a life for a life. But I opened the discussion with outward casualness.

"Well, gentlemen," I said, after a quick mental rehearsal, "there's no disagreement over what the verdict should be, is there?" I did not want to overplay my part. Let them make the recommendation. They might resent it if a greenhorn presumed upon his foremanship.

"Couldn't be," one of the farmer-jurors said. Several others nodded in assent.

I looked around the room. No one offered to speak.

"Well," I said. "Then he's guilty."

The responses were loud, immediate, and confused. The voice of the first juror rose above the others.

"Good God Almighty, bub," he said. "He ain't guilty. He wouldn't of been much of a man if he hadn't shot them fellows."

Astonished and abashed, but still confident, I said, "All right, it looks like we'll have to take a vote." Under Louisiana law, a defendant accused of manslaughter can be acquitted or freed by a three-fourths majority instead of by unanimous decision. I was positive that at least eight other jurors would agree with me.

Two other jurors, the townsmen, voted with me for conviction. The nine farmers voted for acquittal. One of them patted me on the back and said in a friendly way, "Son, you're a good boy but you got a lot to learn. You can't jail a man for standing up for his rights."

When we returned to the courtroom, I, as foreman, reported the verdict. My face was flaming and my voice rough with anger. "Not guilty," I said, and sat down.

The judge, who had once been our high-school football coach, lost his judicial calm. He announced heatedly that he would poll the jurors, which was his prerogative. My name was called first and I answered, too loudly, "Guilty." But the other two jurors, who had sided with me when we reached the verdict, apparently decided that the jury's public decision should be as nearly unanimous as possible. Maybe it was the custom, maybe not. Anyway, they switched, so that the polled vote was 11 to 1. The late defendant rushed to the jury box and shook hands with everyone but me.

Later, after hearing the story of the trial, my father predicted that I would be labeled a "hanging juror" by the lawyers of the parish and would never serve on a jury again. He was right. I never did.

I have never forgotten the outraged words of that juror. *Not much of a man if he hadn't shot them fellows.* They convey completely that attitude toward

51

violence which is far more characteristic of the South than of any other region. Ours was an unusually turbulent parish, but the difference between it and most of the rural and small-town South in this respect was only in degree.

In our parish lived noted feudsmen, murderous deputies, unwritten-law slayers. Some among them had killed more than one man, and most of them had suffered no greater inconvenience than the time lost in appearing before a grand jury. If they had slain their men in fair fight, or even unfairly if in self-defense or to avenge family honor, they were secure in their communities. A familiar compliment was "He'd just as soon kill you as look at you." An esteemed hunting and fishing companion of the older sportsmen was a one-time marshal, a giant, red-mustached man, who with knife or pistol had hastened five men to their reward, three before he became an officer of the law and two afterward. His neck was almost ringed with a wide scar, a mark of his courage, for he had knifed to death one assailant after his own jugular vein had been nearly severed; and he and his friends took great pride in the incident. Men could be elected to public office—and still can be—despite cases of more or less justifiable homicide in their records; but a citizen who had ever backed down when his courage was challenged had scant hope of attaining office.

There were more praiseworthy aspects of this accenting of individual courage. My own father was neither killer nor brawler, but he sometimes carried civic-spiritedness and personal honor to what might be considered elsewhere as extremes. One of my earliest memories is of my father, booted and heavily armed, leaving home nightly for a week or more as a member of a very special posse searching for a feud slayer. The fugitive had shot an enemy from his horse, and since the principals had what we called wide connections, being related by blood or marriage to a great many Tangipahoans, the sheriff had found it almost impossible to choose an unbiased posse. Had the posse included relatives of the slayer, it would only have made routine search; and if kinsmen or close friends of the dead man were deputized, they might not wait for the law to take its doubtful course. So my father and a few other impartial Tangi-pahoans—including a minister who had once been a Texas ranger, a bird-hunting doctor, and a business-man—were sworn in as special deputies. They finally caught the slayer one night, and he actually was sent to the penitentiary, though he was released a few years later.

I remember also a day when a drunken citizen had cleared out a small short-order restaurant in town with some indiscriminate but unmalicious pistol practice. In full possession of the restaurant, he defied the marshal to come get him. The marshal, no coward but unwilling to kill or be killed by a drunk over so trivial a matter, asked my father to go inside and persuade the man to give himself up. Dad walked in, unarmed, and in a few minutes he and the drunk came out together.

This code of behavior extended to the young. If we were cursed or otherwise provoked by boys of our own size, we had to fight fairly and immediately. If an aggressor was older, and we were together, we must combine against him; if we were caught alone by an older boy, we must look around for the nearest brick or stick. In such recurrent cases, the single underlying principle was to fight back. But if a grown man were to curse us, touch us in anger or otherwise molest us, we were to report immediately to Dad. And no man or boy could call us that deadliest of all names, son of a bitch, for in my boyhood it had become neither a friendly, meaningless epithet nor one sanctioned by presidential use.

Because of his insistence upon this code of behavior, Dad's policy of direct action was not always restricted to supporting the law. One fall, when I was twelve, John, my younger brother, went with a group of other eleven-year-olds to the fair. Less interested in exhibits than in the midway's games of chance, he lost all of his spending money at one dingy booth where the object of the game was to cover a red circle with three tin discs. John—and everyone else—found this impossible; so, after he had proved the fact to his own, empty-pocketed satisfaction, he remained in the vicinity of the booth, warning his small friends that they had better shun its temptations.

The operator of the game, angered by this interference, cursed John in the unforgivable words, with spectacular embellishments, and threatened to whip him if he did not leave. My chubby little brother ran home, where my father was in bed because he had broken a foot the day before, and sobbed that the midway operator had cursed and offered to beat him. Dad reached for his crutches, hobbled to the bureau and took from it a pistol, and told mother to drive him to the fairgrounds.

His intent seemed to me altogether proper, and I was worried only about his handicap. John and I went to the fairgrounds with them, and John pointed out the concession and the man. Supported by his crutches, Dad began dragging himself toward the booth. My frightened mother told me to find somebody quick to help Dad, and I ran along the midway looking for some of his friends. But dusk was falling, and I saw no one I knew beneath the dim lights strung along the way. I looked back. Dad had reached the booth. I picked up a hefty tent stake and hurried toward the booth. Before I arrived, Dad, the operator, and the lean-to had gone down together, in one tangled heap, with Dad on top, and I did not have to use the stake. Despite his crippled foot and without recourse to the pistol in his pocket, Dad then and there taught one con man to be more careful of his language in our part of the country.

My incendiary turn came a couple of years later, when members of our two high-school organizations met in a baseball game at the new fairgrounds. Except for one male teacher and a handful of young women teachers, there were no adults present, for it was a more or less impromptu contest. My team was at bat, and I climbed the judges' stand to talk to some girls there. As we watched and chattered in the stand, tragedy brushed close to us all.

A man reeled onto the playing field—a drunken man with a pistol in his hand. Cursing the players, he shouted that he was a special deputy in charge of the fairgrounds, and that the students must leave. An older boy tried to argue with him, and the man pushed a pistol in his stomach. Then, still cursing, he began pointing the pistol at different players, ordering them to remain where they were.

In the judges' stand with me was an older student who had been allowed to drive his parents' automobile. Hastily we decided that we should sneak down to his automobile and drive a mile to town for help. We reached the car safely, but as we circled the roundabout road to the entrance gate, the drunken caretaker saw us and cut across the grounds to head us off. He and the automobile reached the entrance together, for we had to slow down at the gate. I was standing on the running board, and as we drove past the man, he swore at us and struck me a glancing blow with the pistol. The blow hurt only a little, but the cursing ended for me all thought of going for a law officer. I was crying with anger and fright.

"Let's get Dad," I said.

At his office, I blurted out what had happened. Dad was out on the street and in the automobile before I had finished, and we raced toward the fairgrounds. On the way, the older student saw the day marshal and stopped, despite Dad's insistence that he could handle the affair himself. Apprised of what was happening, the marshal got in the automobile, but Dad told him to stay in the car when we reached the fairgrounds and not to interfere. The marshal was agreeable, for in that small town there were no disputes over jurisdiction when a personal issue was involved.

When we arrived at the fairgrounds, the slatted entry gate was closed. Through the pickets, we could see the caretaker, brandishing his pistol at the students, who were now grouped before him at the entrance. Dad jumped from the automobile and ran to the gate. I got out, too, and stood beside him. I was afraid. The man turned toward him.

"Open this gate," Dad commanded.

The drunk pointed the pistol at him, through the gate, and then opened it. The pistol was cocked.

"You get away from here, you—" he began. Dad struck first at the pistol, with his left hand, and at the drunk's face with his right; and then he and a dozen mayhem-minded students were on top of the man. It was a good thing that the day marshal had come along. He finally rescued our assailant-turned-victim, but not before the caretaker also had learned not to overspeak himself or to draw a pistol on unoffending students.

There are other stories I could tell, not of my father alone, but of the fathers of my friends, and of their sons, all of us bound to greater or less degree by this inflexible insistence upon personal retaliation and personal participation in individual or community defense. It is a difficult attitude to outgrow. After we had moved to Greenville, where a thirty-man police force more impersonally enforces the law, my wife heard a prowler in the house late one night when I was still at the newspaper office working on the next morning's edition. She locked herself in the bedroom and telephoned, not to the police but to me; and, although the police headquarters were half a block from our office, it did not occur to me to summon the law. Instead, I took a pistol from my desk—an old Southern editorial precaution—and drove home as fast as I could. The burglar was gone by then, and all we could do was laugh at ourselves for overlooking the police.

And, considerably later, I had a coincidental reminder of my own boyhood. During the war, when I was stationed for a long time in Washington, we lived in one of a pleasant group of apartment buildings in hilly, tree-hidden Silver Springs. There were a multitude of children in those apartments, so many that my two older boys still remember Silver Springs as a play paradise. In another building lived a couple whom we did not know, but whose son was a playmate of my older boy, then eight years old. I came home one afternoon to find my son crying and our Negro cook in a rage. The father of the other boy had chased my son home, threatening to slap him and accusing him of stealing his son's helmet. The boys had identical helmets, and our cook had proved that the helmet in question was Hodding's own; but, she said, the man had gone away "talking bad."

I certainly did not want to fight. Even so unmilitary an officer as I knew there were rules governing the behavior of men in uniform toward civilians. But there was my abused son, and I had long ago taught him just what my father had taught me—to fight fair against contemporaries and to report to one's father any mistreatment by grownups. So I took a chance. Young Hodding and I marched to his pursuer's apartment. I banged on the door. When the quarry appeared, I told him that he must forthwith apologize to my son, and that if he did not, he would have to step outside. My father would not have approved of this compromise, for there was nothing in his set of rules that made apology an easy way out. But the plan worked. That surprised civil servant must have thought I was a victim of battle-shock or otherwise deranged. He apologized hurriedly and profusely and then asked me in for the drink we both needed. Today, young Hod, a victim of civilization, says he is glad it turned out that way. And so, actually, am I.

The Southern society remains frontier in many aspects; and this shared compulsion which validates the stereotype of the "hot-tempered Southerner" stems from a long adaptation of the code duello to frontier requirements, and from the frontier necessity for self-reliance. Personal honor is not as important in the anonymity of the city or in the faceless relationship of urban business and industry. And in a highly organized society, protection of the citizen is rightly delegated to men recruited for that purpose.

But the South's development was not urban. Its social organization was built loosely around the farm, the plantation, and the small town; and behind the white-pillared façade of the mansion, as in the poor white's cabin, lived people who were in actuality frontiersmen. The planter, the overseer, the independent yeoman farmer, and the dispossessed squatter had one common responsibility, and that was to protect what they had, including their good names, against any disruptive force. Neither the remote rural habitation nor the town enjoyed police protection as such in the past, nor can they rely upon it appreciably today. The pistol by the bed and in the holster, the rifle on the wall, the bowie knife in the sheath, the huntsman's shotgun—these were nearer than the law. Across much of the South they still are.

The causes in which they are employed are more limited today. The fear of a Nat Turner, inciting slaves to bloody rebellion, no longer haunts the Southern plantation; but even the telephone and the paved highway are not swift enough for reliance when a drunken tenant runs amuck, a fair or dishonest crop settlement is forcefully protested, or a window is stealthily tried in the darkness. And should a suspicious Negro tenant turn wife beater some night or the honesty of a crapshooter be disputed to the ultimate of a cutting, the planter cannot wait for a leisurely deputy, any more than in my small-town boyhood the householder could rely upon the single night marshal for protection from intrusion.

The communal insistence upon personal courage was in part an outgrowth of these diminishing necessities, but it had also a less pragmatic basis. An agricultural society is by its very nature individualistic, less subject to modification by distant forces, however progressive, and more enslaved by patriarchal tradition. To use regretfully too loosely appropriated a phrase, the colonial and ante-bellum South developed in the cavalier tradition. It is actually not important that there were few gentlemanly cavaliers in fact, and that their high standards of living, their general correctness of behavior, and their personal punctiliousness were exceptional rather than universal. Their mores were adopted and adapted for rougher usage by others who might not be gentlemen of Virginia themselves but whose sons might achieve gentility from cotton and tobacco's despoliation of Southern soil. A Southern gentleman need not have any of a Jefferson's knowledge of the classics, a Randolph's perceptiveness of wines, or a Lee's conscientious observance of *noblesse oblige*. But he must keep bright his assumed honor; and if he perverted the code duello so that its expression was as often the ambush as the challenge, and the knife fight and fisticuffs substituted for duelling pistols at ten paces, he nevertheless maintained spiritual affinity with the past. Witness the killer on trial in a Louisiana courtroom who would not have

61

been much of a man if he had not stood up for his rights.

There are worse perversions, too. A lynching mob and a Ku Klux Klan are expressions not only of racial hatreds, but also of the traditional diversion of the law into the swifter channels of extralegal enforcement. Presumably, a lynch victim is guilty of some crime or other; and the Klan, hiding shamefully behind its masks, flogs petty miscreants of both races. I do not cite this in excuse, for there is excuse neither for a mob nor a hooded coward; but indisputably they are also the warped inheritors of this Southern pattern of direct, personal action. And the men who turn aside the mob and stand against the Klan do so not as law officers but as individual men of honor.

But it would be unfair to end with these shameful manifestations. The profession of arms attracts a disproportionate number of Southerners as career officers and professional enlisted men, and is held in higher regard in the South than elsewhere. Some critics of the South explain and deride this predilection for the military life as simply the result of the relative lack of occupational opportunity and ambition in the South. Walter White, who is the director of the National Association for the Advancement of Colored People and who wears his racial militancy like an angry mask, is among them. But I doubt that economic inequalities are principally responsible; the military tradition, so strong in the South, antedates economic imbalances and will very probably survive them. I might suggest that in a not yet perfect world, a nation requires fighting men as well as spokesmen for mistreated minorities, and that if it is a Southern trait to walk toward trouble instead of away from it, we can find both pride and reassurance in it.

And one last and happier story. Shortly before the Marshall Plan for European recovery was approved by Congress, Secretary of State Marshall was the principal speaker at the annual meeting of the National Cotton Council, held that year in Atlanta. The occasion was a momentous one for the South-wide organization. It happened that the Mississippi legislature was in session at the time, and its members deemed it fitting to draw up a resolution expressing their approval of the plan, General Marshall, the democratic way, and anything else with which Stalin might be in disagreement.

They dispatched a legislator by plane, as a sort of winged mercury, bearing their resolution. And so, before the assembled delegates and General Marshall, this spokesman declaimed the considered position of the legislature of a proud, sovereign, and touchy state. Its conclusion struck a note that must have been reassuring to the Secretary of State.

"The legislature of the state of Mississippi," thundered Planter-Representative Larry Pryor of Washington County, "solemnly warns Premier Stalin of Communistic Russia that its patience is exhausted."

63

6.

Gentlemen, Rise

THE POLICEMAN STOOD at an intersection of Capitol Street, the principal thoroughfare of Jackson, Mississippi, enforcing the city's jaywalking ordinance. Just as the traffic light was changing from green to yellow a male pedestrian scudded across. A few steps behind him a young and lovely woman hesitated at the curb, then started to cross the street, although by this time the traffic light was unmistakably red.

The policeman blew his whistle, and, as she looked over her shoulder guiltily, he waved to her. "Get back here, lady," he ordered.

The young woman returned, anger in her eyes, her stride, and her voice.

"Look at that man ahead of me," she raged. "You let him go across without stopping him. But you whistle and yell at me and embarrass me to death—"

The policeman might have argued the point. Instead, he grinned admiringly and drawled:

"Shucks, lady, I don't care if that ugly old man wants to get his head knocked off, but I can't let a pretty young lady like you get hurt."

The pretty young lady smiled the smile of properly regarded Southern womanhood and said no more. As she crossed the street under the double protection of a red signal and admiring Southern manhood, the policeman winked.

"Best way is to perk 'em up," he observed.

It may be that there are policemen in such faraway and indifferent cities as New York, Boston, and Sioux City who would have acted with equal quintessence of tact when confronted with the problem posed by the pretty young lady. But I doubt it. For in those teeming, alert, and practical settlements life is too real and earnest to permit time out for emulating what must certainly be recognized as Southern Chivalry Toward Womanhood.

Besides, it takes practice.

Let us be analytical for a moment, though it is almost a profanation to dissect the sublime. Here on a street corner in Jackson, in the capital of a state whose true worth is often minimized, were blended in proper measure all of the components of the tradition of chivalry. Here were Beauty and Helplessness and the Armed Knight, Gallantry, Admiration and Protection from Danger, Virtue Triumphant—and, at the last, the wink of Make-Believe.

This happy blending is not achieved by chance. To say that the Southern lady and the Southern gentleman are born that way not only sounds a trifle conceited but also disregards completely the four responsible factors. These factors are St. Paul's admonition to the Ephesian women, Sir Walter Scott's novelized lessons in comportment, the true facts of life on the plantation, and the Civil War and its aftermath. They explain the Southern male's preference for "courting" instead of "keeping company," and his consistent self-deception regarding the nature of womankind in general. They also explain how the Southern female has not only survived such regard but has turned it to her own profitable uses.

It is as simple as that.

Take St. Paul first, for reverential as well as chronological reasons. Speaking to the Ephesians, a people who obviously must have been having marital trouble, St. Paul advised the wives to submit to their husbands as unto the Lord and to be subject to them in everything. This admonition was given and apparently taken in all seriousness; and it was fairly well enforced and obeyed throughout the succeeding centuries, despite some pronounced lapses, eventually becoming a part of the legal codes and even the marriage rites of the Western world. The wily Orientals, of course, had antedated St. Paul by unnumbered centuries.

To continue the scientific approach, it must be stated that the admonition of St. Paul was reflected by husbandly attitudes even in the otherwise democratic young American republic. Its net result was to force wives, and particularly American wives, in those vanished days, to gain through indirection those objectives which they could not attain by the direct approach; and since a devout South clung to a literal interpretation of the Scriptures long after agnostic New England turned to freethinking, Bloomerism, suffragette parades, and a recognition that woman's place is at the typewriter, the sweet wives of the South remained committed to an outward appearance of meekness, obedience, humility, and feminine help-lessness.

Among some unsound and superficial thinkers this has been considered an unjust handicap.

Along came Sir Walter Scott and his prolific imi-tators in the Fair Rowena school of literature. They invaded the South at a most propitious time. The Southern gentleman, having become assured of ma-terial blessings through the happy conjunction of the cotton gin, the slave, and world demand for fabrics, was just beginning to find time to act like a Southern gentleman. Since Southern gentlemen in those days were descended from Old World nobility or, at the least, landed gentry and were therefore chivalrous by heredity, they naturally looked across the seas for their pattern. Assuredly it is a good thing, by the way, that Sir Walter and not the Restoration play-wrights set the style in chivalry at the time.

The Scott system emphasized man's protective re-lationship to womankind, with perhaps a tinge of possessiveness; and on the part of woman a virtuous submissiveness, a delicacy of thought, and a general willingness to concentrate upon the higher things of life, leaving to the knight to tilt against the tempta-tions of the flesh, the devil, and mammon. In one im-

67

portant respect this division of activity was admirably suited to the chivalric South and to both sexes. Southern womanhood was exalted to a pinnacle so high that she could successfully pretend to be unaware of the Southern gentleman's earthy lapses far beneath her.

But not even Sir Walter's genius could obscure certain realities of the Southern scene, and particularly certain exigencies of plantation life itself; hence the third factor in the development of Southern Womanhood and the chivalric notion.

The mistress of the Southern manor was required to act like a lady and work like a drudge. Her lord, who never became quite civilized, remained largely outdoors, riding his fields, fishing, hunting, drinking (but like a gentleman), and on occasion paying calls motivated solely by interest in the physical well-being of his slaves. The chatelaine herself stayed close to home where the real life of the plantation was centered. It was her responsibility to supervise the kitchen, to direct the endless baking and curing and preserving, to exercise over-all care of the sick and to cope with the frustrating ineptness or reluctance of the happy slave. The production of feedstuffs, foodstuffs, and the cyclical money crop rested with the planter, the overseer, and God. But the lady's duties were not so delimited. She was childbearer, supervisor of the home, hostess, nurse for the sick, and spiritual comforter—and she had to fill all such roles while living out the most difficult role of all, that of the beautiful, innocent, incapable, devoted, and obedient wife, the exemplar of all virtues and forgiver of all vices.

It is no wonder that the feminine turnover—or turnunder—was high. But those devoted ladies who survived were, behind their drawing-room manners and engaging adoration, a tough and resourceful breed. So were their daughters and so are their grand-daughters; and what I like best and am most awed by is their ability to make their menfolks think other-wise.

And then, the war. If the plantation housewife's existence was strenuous in the halcyon ante-bellum days of chivalry, it was a nightmare during the war and throughout the dark aftermath. While battle and invasion swirled around them, Southern women lived for the most part alone, in threatened mansion and split-log cabin alike, sharing lonely fear, the agony of loss, and a drab concern with the elemental prob-lem of survival itself. The make-believe of chivalry gave way to the drearier pretense that parched corn and hogback made a fine meal. And out of those harrowing years of the Southern ordeal, the artificial-ity of the past was reinforced by a true chivalry of sorrow, by the affection and respect of man for griev-ing woman, and woman for broken man.

But that was a long time ago, though my grand-mothers did not think so in my boyhood, and the world has since suffered fresher and more extensive wounds. It is worth remembering, however, that while the Civil War intensified the self-reliance of the Southern woman, the Reconstruction period that followed made it imperative for her to hide that self-reliance even more effectively behind a mask of appealing femininity. The self-respect of the home-coming, defeated Confederate demanded that manliness be thus buttressed; moreover, in a very primitive sense, Southern women had to compete with each other for the men they outnumbered. Coquetry, charm, the ability to attract became practical necessities for the woman who sought a mate or would heal a husband's wounds of the body and the spirit. And, because of these imperatives, the South slipped into an elsewhere archaic matriarchy; a competitive, coquettish society which set great store upon the feminine and in which the true role of woman as the pursuer instead of the ostensibly pursued is still enacted with a purposeful skill that is unmatched anywhere else.

These observations, which I had not intended to contain even a hint of seriousness, bring us to Miss Rachel, who died manless at eighty, some twenty years ago.

Miss Rachel lived with us from my babyhood to her death, and we always described her vaguely as a sort of great-aunt. Actually, she was unrelated to us by blood and was linked only by a distant in-lawish connection; but in the South of a generation ago there were many such permanent guests, secure in the

70

clannishness that ordained shelter for the shelterless
who claimed remotest kin.

To judge from the daguerreotype on her bureau,
Miss Rachel must have been a beautiful girl. But
she had never married. The family story had it that
she had loved one man in her native New Orleans,
and he had been killed in the closing days of the war.
There were others whom she might have married,
so the story went; and once in a while my father
would tease her about one of these, a gay ghost
named Witherspoon, in whom she would spiritedly
deny interest and as spiritedly defend as being a pillar
of Dr. Palmer's First Presbyterian Church. That was
her highest compliment for any of her dead contemporaries.

Sometimes, at our insistence, she would tell us of
the occupation of New Orleans by General Ben Butler.
She hated his memory and recalled that she had once
made a face at him, but she admitted that old Ben's
officers behaved decently enough. But I do not remember Miss Rachel now for her girlhood's martial
background or for the perhaps apocryphal tragedy
that left her a spinster. Instead, it is her vigor and
resourcefulness, the steel that braced the posture of
genteel ineffectiveness, which I recall with wonder.

Miss Rachel was up every morning before dawn.
She was the family's unfailing alarm clock and the
scourge of cooks and maids. Owner of a green thumb,
she was in the yard whenever the seasons permitted,

planting, weeding, experimenting with seeds and shrubs and rose clippings and potted plants, independent of the garden-supply stores, for she procured her own seeds and clippings from friends or—so we believed—simply thrust into the earth everything from avocado nuts to banana shoots and made them grow and flourish.

She saved everything; rags, twine, wrapping paper, pins, buttons, medicine bottles, boxes and other containers—and everything she hoarded found eventual use. She would not wait for the periodic seasons for canning and preserving. If there was enough fruit left over from a meal to make just one small jar of jelly or preserves, Miss Rachel would prepare it. No watermelon rind escaped her; and she liked especially to make from blackberries or elderberries a mild wine, which she would sometimes sip sparingly, explaining that she was indulging only for her stomach's sake.

To us children she spoke almost entirely in Biblical or secular proverbs, and they frequently were effective. Even now, I can reel off scores of them. *Enough is as good as a feast. Children should be seen and not heard. Man shall not live by bread alone. Penny wise and pound foolish. Procrastination is the thief of time. Man proposes but God disposes. Fools rush in where angels fear to tread. Satan finds some mischief for idle hands to do. A stitch in time saves nine. As the twig is bent so is the tree inclined. The Lord loveth a cheerful giver. He who laughs last laughs best. Waste not, want not. Cut your garment according to your cloth.* . . . We were thus admonished at every turn, and it was not Miss Rachel's fault that we did not practice what she preached. She tried hard enough.

The little old lady was a resourceful medicator, if a Spartan one. Her stand-bys were calomel, Sloan's Liniment, and mustard plasters, and she knew the bump-reducing virtues of vinegar and brown paper, butter and cold compresses. She hoarded medicines as she hoarded everything else, and Dad used to arouse her with the preposterously funny charge that each spring she emptied the contents of all prescription bottles together and boiled the result for a special seasonal draught.

Sometimes when we thus teased or talked back to her, she would resort to an unfailing tactic. It was cruel, she would say, for us to mock a weak, defenseless woman; and we became immediately remorseful and comforting, for here was Southern womanhood appealing to chivalry.

For all her labors, she was always incredibly neat and cool-looking and unruffled. She never rested, even on the Sabbath; and she conducted a Sunday-school class for small boys with such fidelity that she once received a church award for five years of teaching without missing a single Sunday. When she finally went to that reward in which she so devoutly believed, we mourned a rare spirit whose influence upon us all was as profound as it was unrecognized in its strength. And I know now that Miss Rachel was the Southern woman of a period in which fortitude and resourcefulness and devotion were cloaked beneath the requisite posturings of the weaker sex. "Weaker sex" is good.

My plantation-bred mother was in her own way no less competent, and she took even greater pains to hide that competence behind the ladylike attributes. Mother would never admit to working at anything. Up to the last minute before one of her frequent bridge or supper or club parties she would struggle with the careless Sookies and Effies and Pearls until the final molded salad quivered gracefully and no tarnish marred a single piece of silver. Then she would disappear, emerging in unruffled bloom just in time to protest to the arriving guests that something or other had so interfered with her plans that they would just have to take potluck.

For her, too, the home was the center of the universe, and sometimes a complex one, what with children and dogs and servants and tenants and a husband who never took a waxed floor seriously; and I have never known anyone who could as quickly reduce father and sons to abject surrender simply by pleading the disabilities, the dependence, and the incapacity of woman. Yet, before her health failed, she rode and hunted and fished with my father; and I remember one grim morning when, belying her helplessness, she held off a cursing, drunken tenant at pistol point until a servant summoned masculine help. In addition to what the Army calls "other duties," she found time to teach me at home until we moved to town so that I could go to public school; and it was not my precocity but her perseverance and thoroughness that put me at seven in the fourth grade.

But Mother was just another helpless Southern woman to be protected.

I ought now to present a representative of yet a third generation, but I must be circumspect, not only because I married her but because she is researcher, editor, and consultant for everything I write.

My wife is also a clubwoman, a member of a study group which meets twice a month to listen to papers upon which the authors have spent long months of preparation. Rarely do they pretest these papers by reading them to their husbands, and much less often do the husbands understand or even listen.

During the winter of 1946–47 my wife worked hard on two papers, spaced about six months apart. One related to the poetry of T. S. Eliot, the metaphysical Englishman whose work is, let us say, difficult for the average reader to comprehend. The other paper concerned the military, sociological, and technological significance of atomic energy. Betty read every evaluation of Eliot's poetry and even the poetry itself; likewise, she obtained and digested all that had been published about the atom. I am sure that her papers reflected all that she had read, and I intended all along to read them, but I never found time, nor

75

did she urge me. Most poetry I like, but Mr. Eliot and the atom had alike always evaded me. Besides, Betty was helping me with a still uncompleted manuscript.

Then, in the late spring of 1947, Harvard University gave me an honorary degree. According to custom, no recipient knew in advance who else would be honored. And so it was that I discovered only when the commencement procession began that T. S. Eliot and Robert Oppenheimer were also marching. I sat on the platform beside Mr. Eliot, and only two collections of atoms, known as chairs, away from Mr. Oppenheimer. We chatted learnedly about the weather, while Betty beamed from the audience.

But she did not remind me afterwards how I might have astounded both a great English poet and a great American physicist had I just read two club papers; nor, at a reception later on Commencement afternoon, did she parade her erudition. She was just the little Southern helpmeet, the wife so proud of her husband, every minute.

When the reception came to an end, she had a learned don in tow. As he and I shook hands in greeting and farewell, he said:

"Your wife has been telling me all about you." Then he added, in unscholarly admiration, "You Southerners certainly manage to marry beautiful women."

Southern womanhood had triumphed even over *Murder in the Cathedral* and nuclear fission.

Perhaps it is unbecoming at this juncture to degrade Southern women by speaking of them statistically. But the tabulations of the census takers do list fewer Southern spinsters, bachelor girls, or divorcees, per thousand population, more mothers and more wives whose occupation is given solely as housewife, and I daresay that if such details are included, the list would show fewer neurotics.

It might also show that they read fewer books, though the multitude of women's study and literary clubs in the South provide almost our only link with the great outside world of arts and letters. But an uncanny sixth sense—or perhaps just simple observation—has made the Southern woman aware that the otherwise heroic Southern male is abjectly afraid of erudite females. Beauty unsupported we can understand and appreciate. Beauty and an outward show of brains—from all such combinations we shy away. And, if the achievements of Southern maidens who venture to the far North are any criterion, we are not alone in our preference for the silky-soft, open-eyed approach that begins perhaps with a "I just think that's too wonderful," and ends inevitably with the wedding march.

Not that we are altogether fooled. It may be that we also like to pretend, in an age in which the equality of the sexes, if practiced openly and competitively, has an otherwise unrecompensed dullness. St. Paul and Sir Walter, take note.

And now for a tribute to beauty itself. As an observant traveler to distant climes, I cannot go so far as to say that the Southern belle is lovelier than are all her sisters elsewhere. She just works harder at it, even to the exclusion of other qualities upon which she might capitalize. The Southern woman today is intruding into man's world of business and the professions; but I have yet to meet one of these adventuresses, who, if God has endowed her with any charms at all, will not try to make you more conscious of these than of her sterling characteristics and net worth.

Why should it be otherwise? The Cro-Magnon man had to be lured into the cave before the family unit could emerge as the forerunner of civilization. The true reconstruction of the South was accomplished by the wife and mother in the desolate home and not by force bills or constitutional amendments. And if the ultimate of horror should descend upon us all, there will surely be heard at its end, somewhere in the radioactive wilderness of the survivors, a voice saying with unmistakable inflection and unchanging purpose:

"Honey, I've found some nice bricks for a chimney, but it'll take a strong man like you to stack them up, 'cause I'm just so helpless."

7.

The Case of Eddie Mack

EDDIE MACK, which was not his name, was a ne'er-do-well, a short, gross man who usually needed a shave and who wore almost the year round a hard straw hat and a collarless shirt, the neckband of which was always held together with an incongruous, shiny collar button. His decent, lower-middle-class parents lived not far from us; and their household included Eddie's sad-faced wife, his children, who sometimes played with us, and intermittently Eddie himself. He would walk past our house on his way to work, and after I knew about his secret I felt ashamed and even wicked when I saw him.

The secret, which children whispered, was that Eddie was living on the side with a light-skinned Negro woman whose home in that part of the town known as the Quarters was familiar to many housewives who brought her their lingerie and better linens for fine laundering. They and everyone else knew about Eddie and the woman and about others like them. Everyone condemned him and pitied his family, but no one did anything about it. Some of the best citizens even hunted with him on occasion, and his quadroon mistress—or high-yaller gal as she was colloquially described—never lacked laundry business.

And later I knew other and more respectable Eddies who behaved much as he did, only more circumspectly and with a less single-minded devotion.

As we grew up we came to joke about the Eddie Macks, debating with adolescent bravado the desirability or inevitability of their fleeting alliances. They were surrounded by an obscene anatomical folklore, and we laughed at this flagrant minority while publicly ignoring its existence.

But there were other and less casual stories. About the Negro bellhop in a Louisiana hotel who was a procurer of white women for the hotel guests and whose horribly mutilated body was found in a swamp not long after the talk got around that he received intimate favors from the women he procured. About the Syrian girl who fell in love with a Negro no darker than herself and who, after receiving repeated warnings, saw him shot to death by a policeman who followed them down the railroad tracks one night to their trysting place. About the Arkansas plantation manager whose attachment to a Negro tenant's young daughter lasted many years, ending only when, an outcast and aging, he shot himself in the yard of the small home he had bought for her and their children. About the dispirited Negro teacher who divorced his handsome, easy wife when he learned that her finery had been acquired without cash payments from the manager of a ladies'-wear store. About the middle-aged Negro grocer, well-liked by his white patrons, who deserted his grocery and his family one night for a sluttish white woman and was caught and jailed —for auto theft—in Illinois, where a Mississippi automobile bearing a Negro man and a white woman aroused a policeman's suspicions.

The Southerner, conditioned to such departures from the norm, prefers not to discuss them except as isolated tidbits of scandal or tragedy. But the irrationality of conduct which these stories illustrate provokes the non-Southerner frequently to pungent comment. We are asked why we believe that laws forbidding sex relationships between the two races are necessary to keep them physically apart if natural selectivity or social repugnance separates man into ethnic groups. We are told the obvious, namely, that such laws have manifestly not succeeded in their purpose. We are criticized for the one-sidedness of their enforcement, since the white man is only rarely punished for miscegenation whereas the retribution is sure for the Negro man who is discovered. If racial purity is our objective, we are asked, what is the difference between a white and a Negro offender?

The mistake these questioners make, of course, is to insist upon rationality in the most irrational area of human behavior. The Southern attitude toward interracial sex relationships—and the attitude is by no means restricted to the South—is no more logical than are man's other wanderings through the whole

81

confused labyrinth of sex itself. And there are certain realities, harsh or inconsistent as they may be, which have directed and still govern sex behavior in its interracial manifestations. They go back far beyond the time when the first Negroes were brought to Virginia or when the colonial authorities initially decided to legislate against cohabitation between white colonists and Negro slaves.

It is difficult to state harsh and often inconsistent realities without stepping on the toes both of the dominant group which imposes them and the submerged groups which must abide by them. They afford no pride for the white man nor comfort for the Negro. The unpleasant truth is that the Eddie Macks and the lynched bellhop are joint legatees of that illogical behavior which from the beginnings of recorded history has impelled the males of a dominant racial, national, or even religious group to possess without compunction the women of dissimilar groups whom they have subjected or exploited, while setting apart their own women as inviolate. The pattern of duality is most apparent when the subjected people are economically submerged, culturally retarded, and profoundly different in physical appearance; it is then that one-way travel on miscegenation's somber street is most rigidly imposed. In effect, the dominant males assume that the bastard fruition of their own lust does not endanger ethnic integrity but that any reversal of the relationship debauches and imperils it.

82

Of course, it does not make sense in the abstract. The process of absorption is just as inevitable through the lightening of dark skins as it would be through the darkening of light skins. But the one method has met with tolerance, even sanction, and the other with violent disapproval and raw fear; and at the roots of the contradiction are instincts more real and enduring than race antipathies.

In no ethnic group has this illogical attitude persisted as strongly as among the Nordic and Celtic peoples of north Europe and the British Isles. From those areas came the principal colonizers of North America and the most persistent explorers and exploiters of the past 300 years. The English, the Scotch-Irish, the Germans, and the Scandinavians were far more rigid in their taboos than were the Spanish and French; but they were scarcely less industrious in begetting the half-caste offspring whom they would set apart—as witness the Eurasians of the Orient, the mixed bloods of the African coast and Polynesia and the five millions or more American Negroes of recognizably part-white ancestry. Obviously, there has also been unwitting assimilation when the person of mixed blood is physically indistinguishable from his white forebears.

All people who have been overcome by north-European and British expansion have been the victims of this bitter ambivalence, but none to such an uncompromising degree as the Negro. I believe that this is largely because the white man found the Negro in a state more savage by white tenets than that of any other people whose civilizations he modified or destroyed, and whose vast cultural lag he forthwith explained in terms of race. This is understandable, for even had the pillagers of the Gold Coast lived in an age of sociological detachment, they would scarcely have included anthropologists and sociologists in their slave- and treasure-ship companies. Moreover, the physical and color dissimilarities of the Negro were more pronounced, recognizable, and persistent. Perhaps also, the consistently menial position to which the Negro was reduced by slavery contributed to the contemptuous evaluation. And certainly the squalor in which the Negro masses have lived, the disproportionately high incidence of disease, crime, and illiteracy which has marred them, and their now-vanishing passivity and seeming moral numbness were wrongly but nigh universally interpreted as racial characteristics rather than as the results of racial mistreatment and neglect.

And, perhaps as a concomitant, there has lingered among most Anglo and Nordic Americans a profound and inexplicable fear that the Negro desires—and in the absence of segregation and miscegenation statutes would somehow be able—to merge biologically with a resisting white majority.

I repeat that these realities of attitudes and beliefs are harsh and inconsistent, but they are realities. The American South, more than any region in the Western world, is in its racial concepts the product of these realities.

Nowhere outside the British Isles is there so large a concentration of people of English and Scotch-Irish ancestry as in the South; a homogeneous, long-established people, their roots reaching back to the clannish, blood-conscious Sassenach and to the English, whose quietly arrogant assumption of superiority is an old and often provoking hallmark. Of our approximately 28 million white people, more than 95 per cent have these common origins, admixed with equally inflexible Germanic strains and leavened in only small degree by the subordinated Latin spirit of blood tolerance. Had the masters of the slave South been predominantly Spanish or even French, it is altogether probable that the South's population today would be as fused as are those of Brazil, Mexico, and Santo Domingo. But only a fringe of the South was settled by Latin adventurers, and these soon gave way, militarily and in their interracial patterns, before the Anglo-Saxon and Scotch-Irish onrush.

Among these blood-proud colonists of a hard frontier, the Negroes came unwillingly and in mounting numbers, not only as chattels but as primitives whose cultural inferiorities were interpreted as being related directly to their color. So it was that from the beginning the Negro's servile condition was condoned as proper and even helpful for a lower order of man; and, in order to maintain the system of slav-

ery and to secure divine sanction for it, it was necessary to perpetuate the theory of superior and inferior
races. I doubt that this effort was generally a conscious one, nor was it restricted to the South, either
then or now. And we can hardly blame our forebears
for accepting the theory that the naked Ashanti was
in fact being aided through his forcible introduction
to white civilization and to a limited sharing of Christianity. Even now the question can be argued with
heat and futility and with a more decent intent than
to rationalize a moral wrong.

Inevitably, the possessors had their way with the
possessed, especially with those whose comeliness
was enhanced in proprietary eyes by the blending of
racial strains. Lust, loneliness, brutality, affection itself—who can say in what proportions these emo-
tions impelled the slaveholder to dishonor the slave,
and who can decide now how much reluctance he
met? If the joining of alien flesh was inevitable, so
too was the ancient, irrational determination of the
predatory male to keep his own womenfolk secure
from the subjugated and the nonidentical.

The Negro male, slave and free, was forced into a
baleful accommodation. He could not protest the use
of his women, but, should he possess or seek to possess
a white woman, forcibly or by agreement, his sure
penalty was torture and death.

So it was that Eddie Mack could walk unmolested
along our small-town street, and a plantation overseer could sit with his mulatto mistress and their

fair-haired children in a house of his choosing. So it was that a Syrian girl's Negro lover died beside a railroad track and a Negro bellhop came to his death "at the hands of parties unknown." The psychologist must be summoned to evaluate the complex and related factors of fear and guilt, conviction of racial superiority, tradition and sex compulsions. But even the discerning layman recognizes that all these factors are present.

And it should be equally recognizable that segregation is essentially the product of the Southern male's determination that, except for the illicit and decreasingly condoned relationship of white man and Negro woman, the two races shall not be joined. When a Southerner protests something he calls social equality he really means sexual equality, whether he knows it or not, and his reaction is not likely to be modified by new laws or the repeal of old ones.

From this insistence that there shall be no intimacy on terms of equal acceptance have arisen the social taboos, wondrously complex and having as postulates not only the enforcement of racial separateness but of racial dominance.

Their extent and intensity are largely determined by numerical ratios and the degree of cultural development of the white enforcers. They are most meanly enforced where the white protagonists are least advanced economically, and most sternly where the pressure of numbers is acute. It is more than unfortunate happenstance that those Southern states

87

whose white populations are the most retarded have also the largest Negro populations and resultantly give more emphasis to the extreme emotional expressions of white superiority.

A list of the taboos would be interminable. I can remember my humiliation as a small boy when I answered "ma'am" to someone who asked a question behind me, and turned to discover that the questioner was a Negro woman; and many years later, my inner misgivings when for the first time I addressed a Negro as "Mr." Although there is still a shockingly great likelihood that the Negro servant in a Southern kitchen is infected with syphilis or gonorrhea or tuberculosis, as long as her biscuits and behavior are good she can care for the children and prepare the meals until the bad blood carries her off; but the meals she prepares cannot be shared at a Southern table with the president of Howard University, the governor of the Virgin Islands, or the mediator for Palestine. It is fitting at Christmas time and on other symbolic occasions to give a drink to the yardman, but he takes his cheer standing up and after his employer. We Delta duck hunters find Negro handymen useful and entertaining company on a long hunting trip down river, and we will munch sandwiches with them in a muddy blind, but back on the boat they eat apart and remain inconspicuous. Gullible white and Negro patrons can mingle indiscriminately in the impersonal, foul-tent atmosphere of the carnival sideshow and the midway's

88

sucker games, but not in the theater. If she has the purchase price, a Negro woman can buy hats, dresses, and shoes in many Southern urban shops, trying on, rejecting, and selecting, and the apparel she does not choose will be returned to the shelves for later sale; but she cannot wear her nonsegregated finery to a white church on Sunday even if she wants to. On the other hand, if she is a loved and longtime employee of a white family, she can attend in that church a wedding or a funeral of a member of the family.

In almost every expression of communal living—in the schools, the churches, the parks and play-grounds, the hospitals, the bus and railroad stations, the theaters—the taboos are maintained. Only the white and Negro slums slough off into each other. The taboos are contradictory only in a superficial sense. The determining point is simply that in the inescapable meeting of the races the superior-inferior status must be maintained.

The analytical observer may ridicule the incon-sistencies and detest the human tragedies inherent in this uncompromising bracketing by race; but neither mockery nor protest nor legislation can, in the ascertainable future, change the white South's conviction that racial separateness at the mass levels of personal contact is the only acceptable way by which large segments of two dissimilar peoples can live side by side in peace. Any abrupt Federal effort to end segregation as it is practiced in the South to-day would not only be foredoomed to failure but would also dangerously impair the present progressive adjustments between the races.

More and more today the white man and the Negro are meeting at selective levels. But such communion is by choice and arises from interest in agreed-upon goals; and, more important, it is far removed from those murky human areas in which the feared and the fearing have the same submarginal denominators.

But as long as the white South continues to emphasize the inferior status of the Negro and makes separation synonymous with subordination, it unwittingly gives impetus to the thing it most fears. To the Negro, whiteness must be a contradictory symbol; on the one hand, a desirable characteristic and a conscious or unconscious goal, since without it he is denied the privileges of full citizenship; and, on the other hand, a hateful distinction which identifies his exploiter.

It is inescapably true that together with our uniform insistence upon racial separateness, we have consistently denied to the Negro the most precious intangible which man can possess. That is self-respect. And it is not necessary for the white South to strike at human dignity as a means of maintaining separation. More, it is not only morally wrong; it menaces the very principle of ethnic integrity upon which the structure of segregation theoretically rests.

Put it in the most human terms. In every town in the South there are Negroes who in their physical

90

appearance are indistinguishable from white people. If they remain Negroes, they are subject to the multitude of discriminations that would make segregation intolerable to the militant and sensitive of any race. Certainly it is understandable that they sometimes move away and join the estimated 15,000 white-skinned Negroes who yearly cross over to the promised land of equal justice, unhindered franchise, unrestricted accommodations, adequate hospitalization, equal wage scales, and—so small and yet so great a thing—a handle to their names. Readily understandable, too, are baser and more vengeful attempts to attain the forbidden, and the pathetic success of the manufacturers of hair straighteners, and skin bleaches.

This thrusting toward whiteness is surely motivated primarily by an urge to escape from or avenge the penalties of blackness and not by any abstract considerations of the relative merits of various skin pigmentations. When men meet on equal terms, it is unnatural that any should experience shame because there are differences in physical appearances among them; the shame arises when stigma and subordination result from those differences; and with such humiliation comes inevitably the human urge to escape or retaliate.

It should be apparent that the very real economic and political progress which the Negro is making in the South has been accompanied by a decline in the traditional white man–Negro woman pattern of mis-

91

cegenation itself. The slow expansion of a Negro middle class in the South has brought an ethical consciousness and a race pride that are evident in the decrease of common-law relationships among Negroes themselves and in the decline of *mésalliances* between white men and Negro women. There is no evidence that the educated, enfranchised Southern Negro is any more intent on marrying our daughters than was his slave great-grandparent. Nor, being a realist, does he share his Northern brother's gnawing preoccupation with segregation itself.

I believe that Savannah, Georgia, is an example of almost all the Negro wants now to attain or can now attain as a citizen of the South. Savannah is not paradise, but it offers proof that separation and subjugation need not go hand in hand. The Negro votes freely there although he represents 40 per cent of the population. In 1948 more business licenses were issued to Negro than to white businessmen. Negro doctors, lawyers, dentists, and bankers thrive professionally. The police force includes twelve Negroes and the post office employs fifty-four Negro mail carriers. Parks and playgrounds, schools and hospitals are more nearly equal in Savannah than anywhere else in the South.

I know that this explains the community and regional pride in the voice of the young Savannah Negro, a college graduate, who said to me: "I wouldn't live anywhere else than Savannah. We're treated like human beings here; and when we're treated like human beings, there's no reason for anybody to be afraid on either side."

That is something that Eddie Mack would not understand. But there are fewer Eddie Macks these days.

8.

Clint Ate Corn Pone

CLINT WAS REPEATING the fourth grade, which
was his last, when I caught up with him; and I
paid him little notice until a rainy noon when we sat
near each other in the grammar-school hallway to eat
lunch. I brought lunch to school only on rainy days,
or when my mother was ill or shopping in New Orleans or was for some other reason unable to meet
her children at noon and drive us home for the midday meal; and these rare occasions were almost as exciting as picnics. Our cook contributed to the excite-
ment by packing fried chicken, stuffed eggs, tomatoes,
jelly and cheese sandwiches, fruit, cookies, and a small
thermos bottle full of hot chocolate into oversized
lunchboxes, each holding feast enough for any two
children.

So on that rainy noon I sat next to Clint, who was
not a friendly or popular boy, only because there was
a vacant place beside him on the bench. He brought
his lunch every day because he lived in the country
and there was then no provision for school lunches. It
was also in the days before school buses and he usually
walked to school, though sometimes he came to town

with his father in a mule-drawn wagon, and sometimes he did not come at all.

His lunch was packed in a brown paper bag, and as he reached into it, I saw him eying my full box. He took from the bag a cold baked sweet potato and a hunk of corn bread, that was all, and began peeling the sweet potato. My first mouthful of fried chicken became of a sudden hard to swallow, and to save me I could not look anywhere except at the potato and corn bread in Clint's hands. Miserably, I thrust my lunchbox at him and asked him to help himself.

Clint's ordinarily dull blue eyes narrowed in anger and scorn. "Naw," he said. "Keep your dern fancy fixin's to yourself." Then he got up from his place beside me, walked to the other end of the hall, and sat down on the floor by himself.

I remember wanting to cry. I followed him, a piece of chicken and an orange in my hand, and sat beside him. "Take it," I whispered, "I can't eat all this crazy stuff."

Clint doubled a bony fist. "You get away from here or I'll knock hell out of you." So I left him.

I do not recall much else about Clint. That was his last year in school and we never became friends after that rainy noon. The children would giggle at his inability to recite his lessons and at his habit of putting his head on his arms and unconcernedly dozing in class until the teacher shook him or, in frequent exasperation, tugged at his stringy, white-blond hair. We knew that he was a poor white and that he lived

95

somewhere out on the creek road and that he had a multitude of brothers and sisters. Some of the other country boys, better off than he was, reported that if he and his own family were not clay eaters, it was certain that he had kinfolks farther out toward the creek who were. I did not know then why some people do eat clay.

There were others who replaced Clint fleetingly, in my boyhood's superficial awareness that all was not right in the world. Ours was not a Tobacco Road region, any more than the South is only Tobacco Road; but Tobacco Road ran through our parish too, as it threads throughout the South, and there were and are too many who dwell along it. Clint was one of these, and if I saw him clearly one noonday at school, it was only by accident. We do not see them as a rule, for we are too accustomed to their presence, too adjusted to the factors which create them, too resigned to their perpetuity.

Clint is everywhere in the South today; the man grown from a boy with a cold sweet potato in his hand, a boy with a bitter, twisted pride, his eyes dull and sleepy, his thin shoulders hunched over his desk in malnutrition's lethargy. He is not representative of a majority, but certainly he is at least one in six even now; and if you add to him the three in five who are identical with him except in color, the statistics that represent them become monstrously alive.

Knowing nothing more about Clint himself than I have already written, I can say only that, statistically, he was not necessarily doomed. He could have become one of three persons, and in each projection his children—if he has any—have a better chance than did he, which is a consolation and a beacon.

Perhaps Clint stayed where he was, on his father's worn-out land, or moved down the road to a little piece of land no better. If this is what happened, it is not difficult to follow him after he left the fourth grade, and there is no hope in his story. Clint would have lost his teeth early, and married early, and he would be known now as a lazy, no-account human, because it is so easy to mistake for laziness the sickness that comes from a mosquito bite or a tiny parasite worm or a corn and hog diet, or misery in the back, or the affinity of the shallow well for the privy's deposit. But neither malaria nor hookworm nor pellagra would have hindered Clint from populating a shack with the children borne to him by a girl who became old before her time. He would have become more ill-tempered and quarrelsome with the years, and sometimes on Saturday nights he would get liquored up and make trouble in town. Clint would have wanted to fight when the war came, but the Army would have rejected him for physical unfitness. And I doubt if I would recognize this Clint today if I saw him squatting on his front steps, his overalls slack against his thin body and his blue eyes baleful and suspicious and proud, because he would seem to be too old for the man I knew as a boy.

But maybe Clint was not as unenterprising as we

and the teacher thought. Perhaps he foresaw what he would grow to be as tenant or squatter or owner by inheritance of his father's outraged land, and so decided that he would have none of it. He might have come back to town to work in the box factory where a willing man could make twenty cents an hour; and if he stayed on he would be making more now between the layoffs, enough certainly to live in a somewhat better shack, to eat better, to send his children to the new school, and to vote angrily for the candidates who denounced starvation wages and niggers and such. If he became dissatisfied at the box factory, he might have turned to logging or to day laboring or to dabbling around as a carpenter's helper or whatever work was handy for an all-round sort of man.

And it is altogether likely that the worker, Clint, who had been a farmer, might have become a part of the South's principal export commodity—though he would not have recognized himself as such—after the depression years vanished before the prewar and wartime demand for labor up North. He may be in Detroit or Flint or Pittsburgh or out on the West Coast now, a semiskilled or even a skilled worker, with an automobile and a union card and a cramped apartment for his wife and children, worrying now only about shutdowns and the cost of food. He would not feel lonesome so far away, because he is among friends and counterparts, the thousands upon thousands of them who have trooped from Georgia and Tennessee and Mississippi to the glittering land of good pay and steady work, forsaking or inexorably pried from their bare, gutted fields and their by-passed little villages. They are more favorable statistics now, these roughly minted aggregations of human wealth for which we have not found enough productive use at home. Whether Clint has gone to Detroit or lives yet in the back country that spawned him, he remains an unsolved problem for those who would match the South's abused and polluted reservoir of natural and human riches with the skills and capital and guidance required to make full use of them.

Not that such use is impossible of achievement, or that it is altogether unachieved now. Clint, the one white Southerner in six, may have become the one poor white in perhaps twenty who has triumphed at home over the debilitating environment which fashioned him—and fashioned likewise the mass of Southern Negroes for whom the adjective "poor" is redundant.

It may be that after Clint left school, he did not stop learning, and that something spurred his neglected body and stultified mind. Perhaps he listened one day to a county agent (God bless those men who so patiently and skillfully work for the earth and the earth people) and labored thenceforth to live from and restore his father's small, ravaged farm. This would be no fairy story, for I have seen it come true time and again, though not often enough. Clint may have restored and added to those acres; more likely, he would have moved from them to more productive

99

soil, as a tenant or sharecropper under a man blessed with conscience and ability and fertile land. There are many such landowners in the South, though I would not argue that they are a majority. And, if the crops were good and the settlements fair, Clint may be a renter now or owner himself of a decent farm of his own. He may have found a helping hand in his far-away government, in an agency that makes farm owners of a limited and tested number of the landless and determined. We have more than 200 of these in my own county, and though some of the big land-owners laugh at or mistrust the Farmers' Home Administration, they cannot dispel the reality of the diversified, supervised acres, the painted little homes, the electric lights and refrigerators, the cow pastures and chicken yards and hogpens, the truck gardens and the laden shelves in the kitchen.

But the odds are against the fruition of Clint, who did not have enough to eat and whose body was chronic host to maladies that do not kill outright but sap and enervate the flesh and the spirit too, and shorten life's useless span. There are those who say that we should not waste sympathy on him, that our country was built by men who likewise were meanly housed, poorly nurtured, and untutored, and that whatever ills befell Clint were his own fault. And it is true that men here and elsewhere have risen above environments as hapless as Clint's. It is also true that as offset to each of these, there are the thousands of early graves, the thousands whose dwarfed existences have hideously balanced the extraordinary handful.

And there are those who conversely see Clint as victim of a deliberately cruel conspiracy by which the few may ride upon the backs of the many. But Clint was not the victim of conspiracy, except as men conspire shortsightedly to use the earth and their fellows for the immediate short-term gain. He was the unintended by-product, not the purposeful result; the pattern of his degeneration was begun even before men put the plowshare to the American earth, for the destructive process of denitrification is hastened by the mildness of the Southern winters, so that much of the South's soil erodes even under the best circumstances more readily than does the soil of the North and West. What nature threatened mildly, man hastened. Clint was the almost inevitable product of erosion, the erosion of land and the erosion of people because of the use to which the land was put.

Perhaps some distant ancestor of Clint's was owner of many acres a hundred and fifty years ago when the South began to mine its land in earnest. He may have been a small, yeoman farmer, which is more likely. Or, a failure in the new, open continent, he may have lost nothing from the ravenous development of the cotton economy because even then he had nothing to lose. It is immaterial now. Somehow, somewhere he gave up what he had to a man more able. He moved on. Ahead or behind him came the more able men, with a passion for land and money, owners of slaves who could produce more profitably from their vast holdings than could this long-ago Clint on his fewer and less desirable acres. The big continued to swallow the little, which is not new in the world. Always, it seemed, the Clints were cursed—by sickness, accident, by a weakness for whiskey or gambling, by crop failures and fiddlefootedness, by a reckless uncalculated patriotism—and in the wake of the varying curse, the sons and daughters scattered, some to climb upward, most of them to deteriorate on the marginal lands and the unwanted mountainside, while the cotton kingdom expanded and the kingdom's earth sicklied.

The South was not unique in this process of human development and human decay; the multiple factors which cause some to thrive and some to fail are everywhere. But the South was unique in the system by which it produced its feckless variants and hastened their ruin. The cotton kingdom created and left a dismal white peasantry upon the lands which cotton wore out, and these inheritors of ruin added to the land's destruction. Cotton devoured land and men, requiring and creating poverty as its handmaiden. However morally wrong and degraded his condition, the slave enjoyed at least the kind of concern which is extended to anything of value; but not so the free man who could not compete with slavery, and no one fought a war to make his freedom real. Had there been an Industrial South, coincident with the Cotton South, the dispossessed whites might there have found refuge and security of a kind. Instead, the luckier or more enterprising among them moved away to help populate the Southwest and the West. The least aggressive stayed on to become the principal victims of the war that freed neither slave nor poor white from the system that was more destructive than the war itself.

There is no disputing that cotton has been vital to the American economy, that it precipitated England's industrial revolution, that for generations it paid for American imports and loans from Europe, that it was the raw material which provided the backbone of New England's industry, and that today it affords a direct or indirect livelihood for millions. But it has exacted a toll so great that we can honestly speculate whether the South would not rest today on far more solid foundations if never a bale of cotton had been produced from its soil. The wealth it created has returned only in small part to the South, and the spread of whatever did return has been infinitesimal. It is no accident that the Southern states which have been most completely given over to cotton are the least wealthy and the most backward by every social measurement, and this lag cannot be ascribed solely to the presence in these states of the greatest relative number of Negroes. Even if it could, the indictment of the cotton economy could be no less severe. From the Atlantic to the Rio Grande, cotton debauched the earth and stunted a people's conscience, so that the red, gullied field and the thin-faced boy named Clint came to be taken together as inevitable.

This is less true now, and tomorrow it may be almost entirely false. There is some order in cotton's kingdom and some awareness of responsibility for land and man. Clint's children, wherever they are, do not go as hungry at school as he did. Somewhere near them, if they live outside a town, a school bus runs; and there is a concern with their welfare which Clint never knew, a concern which the olden lords of the South only rarely evidenced. And, even if too slowly, we are restoring the land which spawns the Clints, and putting it to wider and more saving use.

But because it has lived with its Clints for so long, the South looks too complacently yet at the face of poverty and at what trails in its wake; too complacently if only because the Clints, no good at anything else, are good haters, good breeders of more than children, good soil for an unwholesome flowering.

9.

"Those Damn Dagoes—"

THE SICILIANS began spreading through Tangipahoa Parish in Louisiana about the time I was
born there. They were my first "foreigners," a word
that, as I later learned, described all strangers; and
these small, swarthy, hard-working peasants were
strange to us indeed.

My father owned a large strawberry farm which he
operated on the sharecropper system, and as far back
as I can remember we had Sicilian as well as Negro
tenants. Only we did not call them Sicilians or Italians,
but Dagoes, which was not a complimentary designa-
tion nor was it meant to be. There was not much solici-
tude for the feelings or well-being of the Dagoes.

Once my younger brother was joined at play by two
of Tony's olive-skinned children who ventured across
the road for the first time to see what life was like on
our side. After a few minutes he ordered them away,
pointing out with the cruel frankness of a five-year-old
that they smelled bad.

Certainly they smelled different. To them clung the
aroma of garlic and the homemade strawberry wine
which even the youngest were usually allowed to

drink sparingly. Everything about them and their parents was different, so much so that the farm Negroes made unabashed distinction between Dagoes and white folks and treated these alien fellow tenants with a sometimes contemptuous, sometimes friendly, first-name familiarity.

They spoke almost no English. They kept herds of goats, whose milk they drank or used to make a hard, strong cheese. They tended table-vegetable gardens in unbelievably small corners of their back yards. Behind their crowded shacks stood conical ovens of yellow clay, in which they baked long loaves of dark, crusty bread.

My germ-conscious mother forbade us ever to eat this bread; so of course we ate it whenever we had an opportunity, preferring it to the less romantic biscuits and corn bread at home. To cross the road to Dago territory was to visit a faraway country; a land whose shabby inhabitants decorated their cabins with gaudy plaster statuettes and calendar pictures of the saints and covered their beds with riotous red and green and yellow spreads; an exciting world where voices rose in loud unintelligibility at the least provocation and subsided with mirthful suddenness, and where unconscious grimaces and gestures provoked us to delighted laughter.

And once a year there came St. Joseph's Day. Even my mother shared our visits then to the homes of the devout Sicilians who had erected shrines to St. Jo' and offered hospitality to every visitor in return for favors which their patron saint had granted during the past year. On such occasions the pitiful cabins became gay fairylands. Spread out for the visitors' selection were brittle, brightly iced cakes, bottles of strawberry wine, cheeses, fruit, even store delicacies. The walls and ceilings were festooned with red and green ribbons and long strings of dyed peanuts. And flowers everywhere. Flowers and smiling graciousness and devotion, as these strange, humble worshipers opened their homes to their friends and the curious Americans.

On St. Joseph's Day, at Christmas time, and on other special occasions my father and the other landowners would drink the heady, sweet strawberry wine with the Tonys and Angelos and Dominicks and Santos and laugh and joke with them. But most of the time the barriers of language, customs, economic relationship, and suspicion kept them apart.

The native Tangipahoans were indeed suspicious of the Sicilians. They grumbled about those damn Dagoes who would take a cussing as meekly as a nigger, who lived like pigs and hoarded their money, who were always trying to outfigure everyone, and who, they predicted, would some day overrun the country. They said that for all anyone knew the Dagoes were Blackhanders, members of the Mafia gangs like their compatriots in New Orleans who, a generation earlier, had stopped killing each other long enough to murder a chief of police and had finally been put in their places by the lynching of the accused ringleaders in the chief's assassination. That was the way to handle them when they acted up. So the talk went, while the Dagoes grubbed in the strawberry patches, their children working beside them, and pretended not to understand when the Americans jokingly questioned them about what they were going to do with all the money they made.

The Americans found out soon enough.

Not only the landowners looked down on the Dagoes. The Negroes would not accept as superiors these white people who worked so unceasingly and who were so uninterested in relaxing from their labor on Saturday nights; white people who messed with goats and back-yard ovens and vegetable gardens when grocery stores were so handy, credit generally available at the commissaries on the larger farms, and an advance obtainable with only a minimum of wheedling; white people who put their children to work from can't see to can't see, just like colored people had to, and who did not take time out, either the grownups or the children, to play a little.

I remember the first explanation I heard concerning the difference between Dagoes and other people. It came from Ike, an amiable old Negro who worked mostly around the yard and who was the repository of a great and freely shared amount of misinformation. Whenever Ike got ready to deliver himself of an opinion, he would squat on his haunches and begin making circles in the ground with a nail or stick or any other object near at hand. Then he would emphasize his conclusions by drawing heavy lines through the circles, as if in punctuation.

I must have asked Ike why Dagoes behaved as they did. Ike started his circles.

"Dey bound to be different, dat's all," he said. "Bound to be by the Lawd and it ain't dey fault"— heavy lines in the dirt—"and the onliest reason I can see is dat dey got jus' a little too much Injun blood in 'em." More heavy lines. Where that supposition came from I never knew, but for awhile I conjectured that maybe Columbus had dropped a cargo of Indians in Italy on his way home.

The Dagoes were no less unfathomable to a third group in the population, described behind their backs as rednecks or peckerwoods. Few of them in our parish were tenants. But their small holdings were usually isolated and unproductive, and their farming was limited to casual corn and bean patches, an acre or so of strawberries—which in Tangipahoa substituted for cotton as the cash crop—and some lean, free-wheeling pigs known as piney-woods rooters. They were prideful and touchy, and their preference for lethal settlement of disputes had long since given our parish the deserved name of Bloody Tangipahoa. Most of them were churchgoers, but they preferred their back-country, uninhibited meetings to the more sedate congregations in town; and in their politics, which they took seriously, they were intensely partisan and vindictive. And if they did not consider themselves as good as the next man it was only because they

109

considered themselves better, a belief which they were ready to back up at any time, with weapons of choice immaterial.

At some time in the past, somewhere from the seaboard to the Mississippi, their forebears had been squeezed out, or had lazed or sickened themselves out of a more substantial equality; so here they were in Tangipahoa Parish, as they were in Tennessee and the Carolinas, Alabama and Arkansas and Georgia, overtaken Americans, products of the economic exclusion of the plantation, survivors of a host of unrecognized and debilitating maladies.

A mile or so from us lived one such family, better off than most of their cousins, though neither the husband nor wife could do more than scrawl a signature and spell out the simplest words. The father—call him Abel Fletcher—was a lean, tall, unusually erect man, who swore magnificently and indiscriminately at his wife, his children, Negroes, and Sicilians, all of whom were greatly afraid of him. Abel always managed to have a proper saddle horse and liked to ride even for short distances. His other luxury was a broad-brimmed Stetson hat which added to his height, and on horseback he was an imposing and to me a terrifying figure.

There were no similar luxuries for his wife and the children she bore every year. They went barefooted, even in weather that made us shiver; and if they did not work as hard as the Sicilians, they nonetheless always seemed busy with a multitude of chores. The children put in a few years at a near-by one-room

school, but I doubt if the eight of them averaged a
fourth-grade education. Three of them died very
young, and one of the boys, whom my mother described with sympathetic understatement as unfortunate, could not learn anything.

But they never asked anyone for anything; and they
seemed content with their overfull, dogtrot house,
their run-down fields, and their common distaste for
book learning and Dagoes. Once Abel, standing beside my father and watching the Sicilians at work
across the road, summed up his spite against them in
terms that again made me wonder, as had Ike's conclusion about Indian blood.

"This used to be a white man's country," Abel said.
"But I'll be goddamned if it is any more. One of them
smart-aleck Dagoes from Tickfaw tried to buy my
place from me the other day. Son of a bitch if I know
what we're comin' to next."

Old Abel, who must be past eighty, still rides a
horse. The house is crowded now with the families
of two sons who stayed with him. And he has not sold
his land to the Dagoes. But the Sicilians, whom Abel
used to curse—and probably does yet—have bought
land of their own, building homes which are far better than his and making more from the soil of Tangipahoa than ever my father and his Negro tenants did.

For the Dagoes were not content as were we and
Abel and the Negroes on our farm. They had not
come to Tangipahoa Parish in search of ready con-
tentment.

111

Their ascent was at first almost imperceptible. We would learn with unconcerned surprise that Giuseppe Noto had bought himself twenty acres and was leaving to grow strawberries on his own; and my father would grin and say, "Well, you've got to hand it to them." And then we would read in the weekly *Vindicator* that Benito DiMarco, perhaps calling himself Benny Mark now, was planning to erect a two-story grocery building, with the second floor for living quarters, on a lot in Hammond that no one had ever thought was a good investment. We began to see more Sicilians in town, cheerful behind the meat counters and the barber chairs. The younger ones were enrolling in the parochial and the public grammar schools, and they would fight now—as I found out—if you called them Dago.

Before I entered high school, independent Sicilian farmers were forming their own strawberry growers' shipping associations, employing Americans for the administrative and secretarial jobs because their own schooling and knowledge of English was inadequate. Somehow, even in the worst crop years, they put by some money, and they used it to buy land or to build new store-dwelling combinations. They began to populate small settlements of their own, and these were known derisively as "Little Italys." One of the more uncompromising towns in the parish boasted that no Dagoes were allowed to live within its borders. But the Sicilians continued to save and skimp, taking time out only for Sunday Mass, and their acreages and their numbers grew together.

Not all of them were good citizens any more than were all who mistrusted or jeered them. Some made their money in underhanded ways, as blind-tiger operators in a parish that had local option before prohibition and as bootleggers and moonshiners during prohibition. Many of the Sicilian storekeepers disobeyed the Sunday-closing ordinances. Few of them contributed to civic or charitable funds or otherwise lived up to our ideas of good citizenship. But most of them were peaceable and ambitious, and if their Americanization was slow it was in great part because they were excluded from community life.

And today, as the old-timers in Tangipahoa Parish predicted, the Dagoes have taken over.

It was only forty-odd years ago that immigrant Joe Dantone opened his fruit store in Hammond.

I doubt that old Joe ever looked young or that he ever had time either in the old country or here to be young. He was a small, bent man with a heavy, straggling mustache and bright eyes that would dart suspiciously at the youngsters who came to buy his apples and penny candy. In no time at all, he had prospered sufficiently to build a sizable brick two-story building on a corner at what was then the eastern outskirts of the business section.

Old Joe was not exactly an affable man; neither was

113

he one to take unfair customer tactics lying down. The postmaster, during my boyhood in Hammond, had a reputation for penny pinching and extreme care in purchasing, and he liked to get all the extras he could. He was a steady patron of Dantone's store, though not a favorite one, for it was his custom to test the fruit thoroughly by taste as well as by touch before buying.

Old Joe did not like this. And one day, as the postmaster proceeded with his thorough examination, Joe asked him a question that added immeasurably to his reputation and his clientele.

"Mr. Massapost," he protested, "you squeeza da grape, you squeeza da orange, you squeeza da banan'. How come you no squeeza da goddam' coconut?"

His wife worked beside him in the store, finding time also to mother nine children. The Dantone children were among the first to attend the public schools; but I knew only young Joe, the third oldest, and I did not know him well because he was two classes behind me. Besides, like the rest of the family, he worked in the store after school as soon as he was old enough to make change and parch peanuts.

Young Joe was a wiry, tough-muscled boy, and popular, but he had little time for playing with the rest of us, and it was not until I had left high school that he came into his own. When he was a junior, he defied his father and forsook the store for the football field. As he established himself as the best halfback prospect of the season, a delegation of football-minded

114

citizens prevailed upon his father not only to permit young Joe to practice regularly each afternoon but to attend the opening game himself.

Standing on the sidelines as the game began, the little merchant was at first indifferent to the meaningless scramble. Then young Joe got the ball and began streaking down the field. When that play took place, old Joe came to life and raced likewise down the sidelines to the goal, yelling wildly in encouragement. Some spectators say he reached the goal line before young Joe did. And from then on he was a football fan.

Because of his high-school athletic record, young Joe received a scholarship to Loyola University in New Orleans, and there he won three football letters and a degree in dentistry. He returned to Hammond as the first college graduate and professional man among the sons of the untutored alien people who had left Sicily for the strawberry fields. When I also came home to start my first newspaper, Joe and I became good friends and fellow political plotters. And it was Joe Dantone, as commander of the Hammond post of the Veterans of Foreign Wars, who gave me my first invitation to speak in my home town twelve years after I had deserted it for Mississippi. In the interim, he and two of his brothers had collected nine battle stars.

Dr. Joseph Dantone is not unusual in Hammond today. There is now almost no business or profession there in which the sons and grandsons of the strawberry sharecroppers are not represented. And though some of the die-hards still protest the triumph of the Sicilians and mourn for the good old days, they would have a difficult time describing just how these younger, newer Americans differ.

If, as my father's generation complained, "the Dagoes lived worse than niggers," they also farmed like farmers, careful of their soil; and they practiced a thrift which was foreign to too much of the South. They were not restricted by the traditional distinction between what a white man could and could not do without losing caste—a distinction which is as difficult for a rural New Englander, busy painting his barn or repairing his automobile, to understand as it was for the Sicilians.

The story of immigrant success is familiar to most of the country. But the South was almost entirely by-passed during the period of the great European emigration to America, and so its disbelief in the dignity of all useful labor has never been sufficiently challenged since the beginning of its peculiar agricultural economy and the establishment of a mutually debilitating occupational relationship between white men and Negroes.

From our by-passed region too many of our best have emigrated, and to it in the past century came too few newcomers animated by a determination to better themselves in a wide-open land of opportunity. The South of the past was an old, closed, and unpleasantly familiar world to the questing Irish and Scandinavians, the Italians and Poles and Levantines. They were too mindful of the feudal-estate system of agricultural Europe to try to challenge it in America, even had they been wanted in the South—and mostly they were not. In the eastern United States, industrial jobs waited; there were mushrooming cities where small businesses could be established, a hopeful ferment and growth and a more rational acceptance of the dissimilar; in the Midwest and the far West were unappropriated lands to be settled and developed without the frustrating competition of the slave and the jealous antagonism of the great landowner. Everywhere except in the South, the immigrants were sought, if only to fill economic vacuums; and though the first waves of home and job seekers were socially scorned and economically exploited, their children have changed the tune. But the South did not have places for the white peasants and artisans of Europe, for its own peasants were black and tractable and undemanding and its way of life pleasant enough for those who controlled it.

So neither before nor after the Civil War did the South receive the mass infusions of new blood and new ideas that helped to populate and vitalize the North. The ruling white Southerner clung to the planter's disesteem for manual labor and self-denial and the value of experiment, and the poor white and the Negro continued to share an understandable skepticism of the American dream. The South was

117

enervated, not by a soft luxuriousness that sapped
the Roman Empire or even primarily by a war, but
by long exhaustion of its earth and its intellect and
its man power in a doomed struggle against reason
and change. Now, at long last, that enervation has
been arrested and the needed transfusion begun.

It is not strange then that the Sicilians took over
in Tangipahoa Parish, or that wherever in the South
the venturing aliens have come they have generally
prospered out of proportion to their investments, their
hopes, and even their talents. They do not suffer from
the dragging handicaps of amiable tradition, nor are
they bound to the fateful imitation which has caused
the white man and the Negro to adopt each other's
least productive habits.

I suppose that Abel Fletcher was an undisturbed
man, satisfied simply to consider himself better than
any damn Dago or nigger and content with that in-
dividualized democracy of the South which made
him, in those things which he valued, the equal of
my father and any other man on earth. I doubt that
old Joe Dantone or any of the successful Sicilians of
his generation ever achieved Abel's self-assuredness.
Nor do I believe that the breed of the Abel Fletchers
is forever chained to the crowded cabin and the un-
tended patch. It is a tough breed, too, and it has
something to teach as well as much to learn.

But the South has suffered greatly because we had
so little room and so little use for the fugitives from
barren, distant lands.

118

10.

"Just Leave Us Alone—"

T HE YOUNG Pennsylvanian, a veteran who had
taken his basic training in a Southern camp, had
addressed himself earnestly to me for nearly half an
hour without asking a question. The occasion was a
gathering at the home of a Midwestern university
president following a talk I had made to the student
body. I had tried to balance the self-evident shortcomings of the South with the undeniable advances of the
past twenty years.

The young veteran had never been South before
his military service, and some of his own experi-
ences here as well as his more impersonal discoveries
had outraged him. He was as sincere in his convictions as he was pugnacious in expressing them. The
gist of his conclusions was that there was no alter-
native to using Federal force, even military force if
necessary, to bring the South to its senses.

Finally he put his only question.

"Why is it that a Southerner quivers like a radar
screen whenever anyone criticizes the South?"

His simile was too good to pass up. I pointed out
that a radar screen detects the presence of enemy

bodies, and that since so much of the criticism of the South was as violent and threatening as his own, I could understand the warning quiver.

The answer, of course, left him unsatisfied and as determined as ever that the South must be attended to. And certainly it is not a satisfactory or complete explanation of the profound Southern mistrust of outside pressures, even those which are well-intentioned, informed, and sympathetic. But the radar-screen simile does underline the essential element of this mistrust, apart from any considerations of right and wrong. The angry Southern reaction to what is branded as outside interference is undeniably guilt-ridden, however subconsciously; and there are dilatory and hypocritical overtones to the plea that if they would only leave us alone we would work out our own salvation. Yet, the old, disquieting ghosts that haunt the Southern mind cannot be so cavalierly laid.

On the wall of my study hangs one of the John Steuart Curry etchings of old John Brown of Ossawattomie, sword and revolver belted at his waist, a suppliant Negro face close to the grim holster, and behind him a Kansas cyclone knifing down from the darkling sky. The imagery is noble, heroic. But my Grandfather Carter would not admire it, were he alive, for he was one of the nervous young militiamen from near-by Charles Town, who circled the Harpers Ferry arsenal and waited for Robert E. Lee and the marines to come and drag out John Brown's body. To my grandfather, John Brown was an insane murderer and the father of murdering sons, who sought to loose an old horror upon the Virginia countryside; the horror of the slave revolt, the burning dwelling, the ravished wife, and the slain householder. John Brown was no hero, no martyr to my grandfather who sniped at the arsenal windows. Inside as prisoner was Colonel Washington, the first president's great-nephew and the kindliest gentleman of northern Virginia. Dead in Harpers Ferry were three other citizens, kindly, decent men too, and one of them a free mulatto. This was no test of the rightness of slavery, this was murder and rapine; and behind old John Brown's handful of white and Negro followers blew a dank wind from the North, the breath of the Abolitionists, Higginson, Sanborn, Smith, Parker Douglas, and the evil rest, whispering rebellion in the night. These men of distant New England had encouraged and given money for muskets and sabers to John Brown of bloody Kansas, and now the red, fallen leaves of the Virginia October were redder still. So believed my grandfather, no defender of slavery but of his hearth and his state; nor did his opinion change throughout life.

Southern anger and mistrust did not begin or end with Harpers Ferry. A thousand slaves might be docile, but there would always be one to listen to the uncertified stranger; and the Southern white man, counting up the more than two hundred slave uprisings through which the Negro protested his chains, remembered that half of them had been incited by the white conspirator, the fanatic from beyond. For slavery there is no defense, and long ago there were ardent spokesmen for freedom even within the slave South. But rebellion was not academic; rebellion was Denmark Vesey aloose on the flaming countryside, and Gabriel enrolling his thousands in the woods beyond Richmond, and Charles Deslondes, the free mulatto of San Domingo, killing and burning on the road to New Orleans. Rebellion lurked behind the whisper of the stranger, the tract of the abolitionist, the speech in Washington; Southern mistrust of the intervener was born and nurtured in an armed camp, the doomed citadel of slavery, while the voices of sane men within and beyond the citadel were drowned in the loud political trafficking and the heated, vengeful shouting. If they would just leave us alone, said the moderate men and the worried men and the immovable men of the South, together; if they would just leave us alone, we would work out our own salvation. But not with a pistol at our heads and a torch at the door.

The South was not let alone and war is not an abstraction of justice when it is fought among the ruins of a man's home. My grandfather's mistrust of the Yankees, vindicated at Harpers Ferry, was not lessened by the bullet that maimed him at Harpers Ferry. Nor was it lessened for anyone in the South, anywhere.

It is not the memory of lost campaigns that rankles,

but the recollection of the by-blows of war. Long ago, on May 21, 1863, the tiny Brandon (Mississippi) *Republican* rendered an accounting of the capture and sack of Jackson, the state capital, in terms that people remember longest and with malice. I have the clipping before me. The itemization can serve as a composite of things remembered, the intimate things that spell disaster and give warning against the outsider.

"The following buildings were burned," reported the *Republican,* in a hasty extra under the banner "What the Enemy Did to Jackson."

"Green's Cotton Factory together with all machinery and 300 bales cotton. Phillips Factory and all small buildings. J. C. Steven's Foundry. Bailey's cotton shed with large quantity lime, cement, etc. Catholic Church and Rectory. The Bakewell House with contents. Confederate House with contents. R.R. depot and all houses immediately south and west of same. State penitentiary with all its machinery. Flouring mill near Phillips Factory.

"All houses on State street from Shaw's store to Graves' corner, including Green's Baking House, Ambrogia's Grocery, Allen and Ligon and Graves large brick building, with a number of intervening houses. All houses on south side of Pearl street from State street to Mississippi Baptist office; including Confederate Quartermaster's offices; a number of sheds and warehouses near the old depot of the Southern railroad where there were immense stores of cotton, sugar, molasses, etc., and numbers of old cars belonging to the railroads.

"All of the houses in front of the City Hall and Market House except Mrs. Saunders' home and one or two small shops.

"Lemon's Hat Factory, Robinson's Warehouses and General Freeman's dwelling house.

"All of the Fair Grounds buildings.

"The rope factory.

"The Salt Petre works.

"Railroad and city bridges across Pearl River and trestle for several miles on Southern Railroad.

"All shops where government work (Confederate States of America) was being carried on.

"All stores in the city were pillaged.

"THE MISSISSIPPIAN office was broken into and type thrown into the street, the press stand and furniture was broken up.

"Post office was rifled of its contents.

"The Governor's Mansion was broken into and the furniture, including the piano, was destroyed.

"The Episcopal church was entered and entire interior defaced.

"Nearly all private residences were entered, trunks forced open, fine clothing torn to pieces, jewelry, silverware and provisions taken.

"Captain Louis Julienne's Book Store, Dr. Knapp's Dental office, J. W. Gray and Company Dry Goods Store, E. Virden's store with great loss of molasses, sugar, etc.

"Busick's Commission House.

"Allen and Ligon's Merchandise of books, papers and money.

"Dr. S. C. Farrar's carriages and horses and Mr. J. M. Rawlins' carriages and horses.

"Almost all cows and horses in the city driven off along with between 300 and 500 slaves."

I am not writing a history of slavery or of the Civil War or Reconstruction, but the folklore of interference which each of these tragic passages produced in the South must be comprehended. Certain latter-day interpreters of Reconstruction seek to prove that only the adamant Southern Bourbon objected to the political and social upheavals which marked it, and that the Southern poor white and the Negro entered into a proletarian alliance which was destroyed only through their desertion by the erstwhile liberators from the North. That I doubt, and while my own doubting may be immaterial, I can say with a conviction born of youthful listening to a wide assortment of my elders that few white Southerners—poor white, yeoman, or aristocrat—who went through Reconstruction relished the experience. Neither "scalawag" nor "carpetbagger" is a nice word yet in the South, and I am inclined to believe that only a relative few of the original specimens who were so labeled were any nicer than the epithets. The South does stubbornly overlook the hundreds of devoted Northern men and women who came South after the

125

Civil War to do their honest best for both races, to establish and teach in public and private schools for the freed Negro, to enter into legitimate business, to heal and preach, and to seek sincerely the political resurrection of the South. But their shadows and their memories were obscured and their numbers were dwarfed by the circling buzzards who swooped down upon the prostrate body, by the cotton thieves and political plunderers, the tax ghouls and berserk comminglers, exploiting not only the prostrate Confederacy but the bewildered Negro.

Yet that also was a long time ago, seemingly too long to influence the Southern mind today. And perhaps the interloper would have been forgotten if his determination had waned after the failure of the Force Bills. But it did not; rather, the continuity of angry intervention has been maintained even to the present. Remember, I am not defending those injustices and contradictions which have moved the non-Southerner to protest and to demand abrupt, forcible, and federally directed change in the unwholesome scene. But I do say that the emotional intensity, the frequently political motivations, the unrealism, and the regional ignorance of so many of the protesters have produced inevitably the radar-screen reaction.

When the late Senator Bilbo ran for re-election in 1946, he was not, in the early weeks of the campaign, a certain winner despite the political insignificance of his opponents. A great many Mississippians had been shamed by his conduct in the Senate; a great many more had never had any use for him during his long, up-and-down career in state politics. Bilbo could have been defeated that year had his candidacy not become a national issue.

Admittedly, the election of a United States Senator anywhere is of concern to Americans everywhere, for a Senator's decisions affect the entire nation. Every citizen had a right to be disturbed at the prospect of The Man from Mississippi returning to Washington to write more "Dear Dago" letters, to revile Jews, and to indulge his blatant racism in the principal forum of the world.

But, the outsiders who desired his defeat made certain his victory. Into Mississippi cascaded the scornful comment of the nation. Free-lance writers scurried from New York on quick, sure-fire assignments. The great national magazines of fact and opinion had a field day. The National Negro Congress, in annual session, demanded that Federal bayonets encircle the Mississippi polling booths, a remindful ultimatum which alone guaranteed Bilbo's triumph. Marchers in the Communist May Day parade in New York carried banners proclaiming that Bilbo and Rankin must go. A conglomerate of organizations won fleeting publicity by insisting in advance that the Senate should nullify the decision of the electorate of a sovereign state.

And on the street corners of Mississippi, citizens

who had never in their lives voted for Bilbo announced heatedly that they were going to help elect the little so-and-so just to show the damned outsiders that they could not run a Mississippi election.

Nor is such unintelligent interference isolated. Let a measure be proposed for Congressional repeal of the poll tax in Federal elections and almost invariably a Northern Negro officeholder or publicist will announce that when the poll tax is abolished he will come down to Mississippi—or Alabama or South Carolina—and run for governor or the Senate. He would not actually try it in the first place, and residential qualifications would bar him in the second; but the stupid, meaningless threat is always enough in itself to rally the affected citizenry behind an equally stupid and meaningless voting requirement.

I will pass lightly over Henry Wallace, who brought about the destruction of eggs deserving of a better fate. His invasion of the South was too patently deliberate to anger anyone greatly, and I am sure that he must have been crestfallen at the calm with which the South and the nation at large received his message. Even so, he contributed nothing but discord when he declaimed that in the apathetic audiences he had seen the evil face of Fascism.

Perhaps the most irritating of all invaders are the investigators with books or articles in mind. But it is unfair to brand them all with the same iron. The contributions of capable sociologists and economists to an understanding of the South have been too readily minimized by Southerners, most of whom never read the scholarly, tedious, and painstaking studies that in the aggregate are helpful. The true student's reading public is limited, everywhere, and his honest purpose is too readily suspected by the Southerner, whose misgivings are easily aroused at the sight of the white stranger in unrevealed conversation with the Negro. Almost every scholar whom I have met while he was engaged in a Southern study has commented upon this mistrust. Almost all of them have been accosted at one time or another by suspicious white men who want to know what they are up to and who are not satisfied until they are vouched for. And here again is the old fear, its guilt aspects as apparent as its roots are deep. *What are they up to? They're stirring up trouble. Why don't they leave us alone to work out our own salvation?*

The serious investigator had an additional handicap in the more widely disseminated product of the hit-and-run school of popular writing. The national magazines are less culpable now than they once were, but the Southern pasture is still green for the irresponsible, mischievous, and shallow reporter, pamphleteer, and writer of fiction.

The national Negro newspapers belong in a special category. They can be properly defended as an inevitable expression of the other side of American racism; they make no pretense at being objective or unbiased, and they are not unique in directing their columns to the lowest levels of literacy and social comprehension. But the isolated white farmer and small-town Southerner, chancing upon a discarded copy, is not inclined to be judicial in his appraisal. The provocative news stories, columns, and editorials are not discounted as the inevitable result of discriminations—and perhaps an entrenched interest therein —but as fomenters of discord. Again it is the outside, and a particularly resented outside, busily engaged in pricking old sores and goading the sufferer. I happen to be a close reader of the Negro press. As a newspaperman, sensitive also to censorship, I defend both its right and its essential motivation. But if I were asked for editorial consultation, I would suggest that the almost unrelieved bias be balanced with a greater recognition of impartial fact and hopeful change. If this could be achieved, the many in the South who are likewise concerned with injustice would fare better in their attempts to defend and to interpret these gaudy, printed spearheads that now so ably frighten and embitter.

The cataloguing of specters soon becomes monotonous and so does the explanation for them. If all were well (we are told), the fearsome wraiths would vanish. Incontrovertibly, all is not well, nor will it be within the ascertainable future. But an imperfect condition does not justify superficial and punitive appraisal.

In the spring of 1948, a Pittsburgh newspaperman shaved his head, acquired a Florida suntan and a cap —God knows why the cap—and, assuming that this make-up would enable him to pass as a Negro, embarked upon a brief, circumscribed tour of the South under the guidance of a representative of the National Association for the Advancement of Colored People. His ensuing stories were syndicated under the intriguing but hardly detached title "In the Land of Jim Crow."

The magazine *Time* welcomed this series with a full-page laudatory digest of its contents. It appeared without qualifying preface in a considerable number of non-Southern metropolitan newspapers. Walter White recommended that the author receive another Pulitzer prize; a publishing house quickly arranged for its appearance in book form; and a new foundation for the recognition of labors in the field of racial betterment subsequently chose the intrepid venturer as the recipient of its first award.

It so happened that I was asked to write an answering series by one of the newspaper editors who had bought these syndicated articles. He sent me advance proofs of the articles. It is impossible to communicate the sensation of moral nausea they produced.

Deliberately or by direction, the author had produced as venomously one-sided, exaggerated, and pugnacious an interpretation of a region and its sins as has ever been published in American newspapers. Amazingly, its content was questioned by only one newspaper of the fifteen or more which printed it: the Providence (Rhode Island) *Journal,* whose editor Sevellon Brown, Jr., suggested that I write about the other side. Of those fifteen non-Southern, metropolitan newspapers, five declined to print my rebuttal.

Aside from the personal emoluments gained by the disguised Pennsylvanian and the increase in circulation which his newspaper may have recorded, only harm resulted from the stunt. A great many people, North and South, were embittered for contradictory reasons. There was already bitterness enough and to spare.

I know that much of this Southern resentment against distant criticism is dishonest. It is probably strongest among those groups which most deserve it, and its base is more emotional than rational. We in the South have no right to say that what we do is no affair of the rest of the nation. An unpunished lynching mob is an affront to humanity everywhere. So is the persistent and calculated denial of constitutional rights to any segment of the population. I am sure that the demagogue is louder in his denunciation of Federal pressures than is the troubled student of government who is rightly unconvinced that the greatest good for the greatest number can be achieved through the emasculation of state sovereignty and state responsibility. Moreover, in the resentful Southern chorus are too many voices whose protests cloak an entrenched economic interest in the submarginal *status quo.*

Yet this protest extends beyond the emotionally

resentful atavist, the calculating political mountebank, and the conservative apostle of unhindered exploitation. The white South does have a historic and a present-day basis for suspicion and fear. The Southern contradiction of democracy is the only one in the nation against which an aggressive demand for full, abrupt, and forcible revision is continuously directed. Ours is the only region in which an ethnologically distinct, repressed, and culturally retarded people are constantly told, through every available medium of communication, that the dominant majority is unqualifiedly evil in its behavior toward them. Certainly this majority is too reluctant to give ground. No one is more aware of this reluctance than the mounting numbers of Southerners who are determined upon absolute justice for the Negro. But they are equally aware that justice and equality and democracy are absolute nowhere in the United States, that the battle line is nation-wide, and that violent propulsion toward the ideal precipitates violent reaction.

Maybe I am just trying to say that there are other ways than John Brown's way. In retrospect, he is Curry's magnificent figure, the liberator of the enslaved, the dreamer of an American dream of freedom. But not to my grandfather. In John Brown's wake, and partly through the opposing frenzies he inspired, strode war; and the way of war was not magnificent to those who survived in its wreckage and for a while stood helpless while the jackals prowled. The jackals have not retreated, either in a Mississippi or a New York; and their contrary, irreconcilable howling again shuts out the reasonable voice.

And this muted voice has something to say: *We have not gone far enough or fast enough, but we have already gone far. Your prodding has been in a measure responsible but not in principal measure, or so we believe. We are not dealing in abstractions here. We know the meaning and the force of spectral fears and we are vying against them with unadmitted success. We will join you in the attainable. But if John Brown comes again there will be furious men to face him. If the imprecations of Garrison and Sumner and Stevens dominate elsewhere, there are as uncompromising Southern voices to contest them. If the spoilsmen of Reconstruction live in the political opportunists of the bloc vote, they can find their shameful match on the Southern hustings. It is not that we must be let alone, but that we must not be set apart as an incomprehensible, stubborn contradiction.*

II.

The Crazy-Quilt Pattern

I CAST MY FIRST vote for President in 1928, when thousands of Southerners were preparing to desert the Democratic party to prevent the Pope from escorting Al Smith into the White House. Convinced that the Brown Derby would not be replaced by the papal zucchetto, and for less negative reasons as well, I was an Al Smith Democrat. So was my father, though with some misgivings.

Because this was to be my first trip to a voting booth, Dad made quite a ceremony of it, and insisted that we go into the city hall together. As we entered, we fell in with a close kinsman who throughout the summer and fall had been loud in his denunciation of the Catholic plot and equally vociferous in his determination to vote for Herbert Hoover. The three of us went inside together. When we rejoined each other, my father said jokingly to our relative: "Well, how does it feel to be a damn Republican?"

The kinsman looked sheepish. "I couldn't do it," he confessed. "I've been stamping that Democratic

135

rooster all my life and I did it again. But I hope that papist ward heeler gets snowed under."

Seventeen years later I was engaged in two equally quixotic and futile enterprises. One was the publication of a minute daily newspaper in Hammond, Louisiana, shrilly dedicated to the extermination of Huey Long's political machine. The other was a campaign for election to the Louisiana House of Representatives.

A bullet ended Long's life in October, before the violent gubernatorial and lesser campaigns were well under way. But his heirs were strongly entrenched, and after the assassination they rode high on the wave of his martyrdom. There were no niceties on either side. The Long machine, still intact, had its tremendous pay rolls, complete control of the election officials and of all state, county, and municipal jobholders, apparently inexhaustible funds, and a record of material achievements that had gratified the mass of the people while enriching the corrupt inner circle. Our ill-assorted and bumbling opposition had, in addition to anger at democracy's long negation, one practical political asset. The New Deal administration, whose enmity Long had earned, was with us— at least at the beginning. Before the Louisiana elections, the New Deal's own practical politicians made a shameful trade with Long heirs, and all was forgiven on both sides. But that trade was not consummated until later; and so, in the fall, the anti-Long organization received a go-ahead signal for the use of WPA work-relief orders for political purposes.

The anti-Long candidates were allotted work-order slips in proportion to the importance of the posts they sought—and their probable chances of winning. My own package was small on both counts. The candidates were to hand out the slips where they would do the most good. It was simple and shameful trading in misery, and the only possible excuse for it was that we were fighting fire with fire.

The word got around quickly that the anti-Long candidates were dispensing this meager manna, and my newspaper office was filled with a succession of ragged, jobless men. I would like to think it was idealism that kept me from extracting vote pledges from these derelicts of the depression. But I am sure it was just plain realism. I knew that pledges of support were valueless under such circumstances, and I felt dirty for even thinking of telling them that I was the white hope of Tangipahoa Parish while handing out a ten-dollar work order. So I just gave the slips away to everyone who came for them. Some thanked me, and a few said they were going to vote for me.

But the only one whose face I remember was a decrepit, middle-aged man in overalls who looked savagely at me and said peremptorily, "I want one of them work slips."

I handed it across the counter.

"Don't get the idea I'm goin' to vote for you, bub," he spat. "I got as much right to one of these things as the next man, and I'm votin' Long right down the line. He give us poor people what we got comin' to us, and I don't give a damn if he got plenty out of it too. All we ever got from the big shots before was promises."

A year later I came to Mississippi. Here Alfred H. Stone is the epitome of the elder statesman. Scholarly sociologist and historian and one-time planter who saw his acres only when he lifted his eyes from his books, he is, at seventy-eight, the able chairman of the State Tax Commission. In or out of power, Mississippi's political factions leave him completely alone, because if they sought to meddle he would quit.

When Mr. Stone was a twenty-year-old law student, he attended the fateful state constitutional convention of 1890, at which white Mississippians turned from extralegal to legal devices to ensure their political control of the state. At that time more than 65 per cent of the state's population was Negro. Today he is the only man still living who attended all of its sessions.

In the winter of 1947–48, when the civil-rights turmoil was just beginning, I heard him give a frank and lucid account of the convention's procedures and objectives. I wish his audience had been wider.

Most of the delegates were Confederate veterans, Mr. Stone said, but there was one Negro delegate. He was Isaiah T. Montgomery, a one-time slave of Jefferson Davis' brother. As a member of the franchise committee, he supported the constitutional changes. Mr. Stone recalled that Isaiah Montgomery "believed that the white people, if let alone, would do the right thing."

So, the delegates set about changing the state's constitution. They had to move carefully, for the so-called Force Bill, sponsored by Henry Cabot Lodge of Massachusetts, had been passed by the House of Representatives.

As Mr. Stone put it, the convention did not attempt the impossible. It did not try to disenfranchise the Negro as a Negro. That could not be done, because the Fifteenth Amendment had been too carefully drawn.

Instead, to reduce the potential Negro vote, the convention took into consideration the behavior patterns that then principally characterized a people only thirty-two years from slavery. Because of the great number of illiterate whites, no educational qualification for suffrage was adopted. Instead, the new constitution provided that a voter must be able either to read *or* understand the constitution or give a reasonable interpretation thereof. Because of the Negro's migratory habits, the convention required that a voter must have lived two years in the state and one year in the county in which he cast his vote. Since bigamy and petty thievery were common among Negroes, bigamists and petty thieves were barred. And payments of poll taxes for two consecutive years were required because of a justifiable belief that the Negro would not want or remember to pay out his money for a nebulous, future privilege. It was not the Negro

139

but his characteristics that were legislated against,
Mr. Stone explained. Legal equity was provided by
making the rules apply to both races. Some of the bars
worked and some did not.

This is Mr. Stone's explanation of the constitutional
provisions for voting, and he was there.

I was especially interested in the attitude of the
lone Negro, Isaiah T. Montgomery, who believed that
the white people would do the right thing for his race.
He was an unusual man. Educated by the Davises, he
became during the Civil War a protégé of the Union
Admiral Porter and was present at the battle of Grand
Gulf and the fall of Vicksburg. During Reconstruction he was a political leader among the Negroes,
and eventually purchased the Davis plantation. He
founded the all-Negro town of Mound Bayou, Mississippi, which still exists, and during the harrowing
Reconstruction period he was trusted by the opposed
leaders of both races.

This much I had already known. But by coincidence
there appeared, about the same time Mr. Stone gave
his intimate account of the convention, a little post-
script to history. It was written by Roscoe Simmons,
the Negro historian, and has to do with what came
later.

Montgomery, it revealed, spoke in defense of the
new voting qualifications that disenfranchised most
of the members of his race. For the sake of peace in
a state, "where every acre represents a grave, every
furrow a tear," he endorsed the new constitution

140

though aware of its immediate intent, for he trusted the white people.

"The alien sought and obtained our confidence but not our affection," Isaiah Montgomery said. "That, Mr. President [of the convention], remains with you. I stand here to present to you an olive branch of peace. It is a fearful sacrifice laid upon the burning altar of liberty.

"I wish to say to my people, nay, we have not taken away your high privilege, but only lifted it to a high plane and exalted the station of the great American birthright. I wish to say to them that the sacrifice has been made to confer the great boon of political liberty upon the Commonwealth of Mississippi."

And then the stinging epilogue. Roscoe Simmons writes that years later, "when Montgomery's people under the new constitution had been reduced by the Democratic party to political serfdom, and what seemed eternal darkness had settled over them, Montgomery was asked, 'Now what of your white people?'"

"Not my white people," the old man replied. "My white people and their chivalry and honor vanished long since from these unhappy scenes and I shall soon join them."

During his campaign for re-election to the United States Senate in 1946, Theodore G. Bilbo spoke one night in early summer at Leland, eight miles from Greenville. I drove over to hear him. The small city hall in which he appeared was overflowing. I stood outside where loud-speakers violated the soft night with his harsh, disembodied voice.

At the edge of the outdoor crowd, a few Negroes stood under a street light, listening with apparent unconcern to Bilbo's strictures against their race. He was at his foul best. Because he was in my home territory and I had written much about him that he had reason to resent, The Man came back at me. I had recently been honored with an award that is prized by newspapermen. Bilbo had an explanation for it: "No red-blooded Southerner worthy of the name would accept a pulverizer prize given by a bunch of nigger-loving Yankeefied Communists for editorials advocating mongrelization of the race."

The stanchly unmongrelized audience yelped approval. Bilbo turned to more inflammatory targets. The niggers were trying to vote, he said. But Mississippians would know what to do. The time to handle that problem was the night before election.

And there had been vile accusations that he was bigoted.

"A young girl reporter up there in Washington came up to me the other day and asked me if I was anti-Semitic," he confided. "That means anti-Jewish. I told that young lady that I was for every damn Jew from Jesus Christ on down."

Behind me, a countryman's hoarse, whiskey-fortified voice punctuated the pause.

"Pour it on 'em Bil', we're with you, pour it on."

And Bilbo, whose worst offense was that he knew better, kept pouring it on for the benefit of those who did not.

The States' Rights Democrats met in Jackson, Mississippi, in May, 1948, to form a permanent organization prior to the national party conventions. The municipal auditorium was decked out in American and Confederate flags. Delegates sat under state banners. Pretty girls pinned States' Rights buttons on delegates and spectators alike, allowing no refusals. Newspapermen buttonholed politicians and politicians buttonholed each other, shouting above the strains of "Dixie" and acting altogether like good Democrats or good Republicans.

The principal address among too many addresses was made by Governor J. Strom Thurmond of South Carolina, who was to become the presidential candidate of the States' Rights party. Young Governor Thurmond was an angry and dedicated man. The South's Democrats, who were the true Democrats, had been betrayed in the house of their fathers, he rasped, and they were determined to punish the betrayers. He recalled with pride—and with historical accuracy—the role of Southern statesmen in the building of the nation. He reviewed the burdens of Reconstruction and inveighed against freight-rate differentials and the refusal of the South's critics to give any credit to the South for anything.

143

In these matters Governor Thurmond stood on firm ground, and, for a keynote address, his was, up to a point, surprisingly temperate.

But when the governor turned his guns upon the civil-rights program, riddling its proposals one by one, he could not withstand the ancient temptation.

"These big machine bosses and their puppets in office, as well as those who think everything can be done by a law from Washington, should once and for all realize that on the question of social intermingling of the races, our people draw the line. And all the laws in Washington, and all the bayonets of the Army, cannot force the Negro into their homes, their schools, their churches, and their places of recreation and amusement."

I had read the civil-rights program in full. I was suspicious of its motivation and doubtful of its wisdom and efficacy. But I had found in it no demand for forcible social intermingling of the races in the South. Somehow Governor Thurmond had, at least for convention purposes.

And so, even though he absolved the Southern Negro from complicity, he summoned about him the cruel, terrible specters, the old bitter ghosts, while furious men cheered their defiance of the unforgotten bayonets of the North.

Here is a final story. In holding it for the last, I have purposely violated chronology.

I attended the funeral of Huey Long in October,

1935, though not as a mourner. The event was macabre. The body lay in state in the skyscraper capitol where he had made unwitting rendezvous with death. And there, thousands and thousands of Louisianians who had believed in this dynamic, despotic man filed in sorrow past his bier, choking the capitol grounds and the narrow streets of Baton Rouge, so that there was no semblance of traffic order, only a surging chaos that reflected the bewilderment of the bereft, hoodwinked people of Louisiana.

One of his lieutenants had been chosen to preach the funeral oration. His hold upon the trusting Louisiana majority had been surpassed only by that of Long himself. He was Gerald L. K. Smith, an unconscionable opportunist, a preacher turned political jackal, who was president and national organizer of Long's fantastic Share Our Wealth clubs. Smith was a powerful orator in the camp-meeting tradition, and it is probable that he genuinely loved the dead man whom he had come to praise and bury. But his words did not need to rise from his heart to have meaning for his listeners, for the meaning was already in their own hearts and this hard adventurer only echoed it.

"His body shall never rest," cried Gerald Smith, "as long as hungry bodies call for food, as long as lean human frames stand naked, as long as homeless wretches haunt this land of plenty."

There was the lesson and the unended threat. But in the South too few who seek to lead seem to be aware of either.

These stories are pieces in the crazy quilt which covers a politically sterile bed. In it lie strange bed-fellows, Bourbon and poor white, demagogue and conscientious citizen. They kick at each other beneath the covers, but rarely do any among them leave the bed, and when they are afraid they pull the crazy quilt over their heads together.

For the crazy quilt's only usefulness or meaning or design is protective. The thread that joins the pieces together is a common insistence upon white political domination in the South, and it is as unbreakable as anything woven by the mind of man.

And so, men who elsewhere would be Republicans or Socialists or Farmer-Laborites or even Democrats all call themselves Democrats here. Their differences become ideological only when a Huey Long emerges in the factional strife. Their principal tenet, which he violated, is that their solidarity can be most securely cemented by what are called safe men, which is to say conservative men. And that conviction, which goes back a long way, is to blame for the South's political lethargy. It stems from a caste system in politics, a system that preceded the Civil War and was intensified in the Reconstruction period which followed that war.

From the beginnings of Southern statehood, the triumvirate of planter, lawyer, and financier—and if it had a military tinge so much the better—has essayed to rule its fellows, though not without frequent rebellion. Occasionally this ruling caste pro-

146

duced its own revolutionaries, as with Thomas Jefferson, though not latterly. Its representatives suspected the less privileged and particularly those leaders whom the less privileged produced; and they failed long ago, though without knowing it, because they forgot the obligations of their emasculated tradition of *noblesse oblige.*

Tom Watson, the first of the Southern demagogues who successfully challenged caste rule, drew poor white and Negro together for a while under the raging banner of Populism; and Populism failed in the South largely because this union by interests instead of by race was a target his enemies could not miss. Tom Watson sought to retrieve his power by beating the race-baiters at their own game, and Populism died even as he achieved evil success.

The demagogues who followed him did not make his mistake.

If they appealed to the honest resentment of the poor and the ignorant and the frustrated against the indifference of the entrenched, they made sure that they spoke to and for the poor of their race alone. Of all the Southern demagogues, only Huey Long did not make the Negro a whipping boy.

But neither the demagogue, thriving upon the needs and the cupidity of the masses, nor the Bourbon who still gives him battle can be blamed for the beginnings of this militant political indivisibility. Had the North been less vengeful and more rational in victory, it would not have disenfranchised the de-

147

feated enemy and enfranchised the free, unready Negro. There was the compounded error. When it was made and militarily implemented, white solidarity, white resistance, and white retaliation became inevitable.

But the inept North cannot be blamed for the rank flowering of the Southern demagogue since Reconstruction. The number of decent, honorable men in public life in the South at least equals, I believe, the despicable stereotypes. Yet their own goodness is too often negative, contributing little to the establishment of progressive social and economic thinking in the South. And they almost invariably meet defeat when they come to grips with the demagogue aware of the resentful mass. They are too often the safe men, the careful men, reluctant to challenge the old order of *laissez faire*. Nor, fearing political suicide, will they challenge the demagogue in his race-baiting. There are exceptions, of course; a Kefauver in Tennessee, a Lister Hill in Alabama, an Arnall in Georgia, a Scott in North Carolina, and their numbers are growing—but they are still exceptions.

The States' Rights uprising is a case in point. It was, at its best, a reaffirmation of the constitutional principle of division of state and Federal powers. It should not be scornfully dismissed simply as a reaction against national concern over interracial injustice or as a Bourbon protest against social advance. But even the worthiest among its leaders did not positively acknowledge that states' responsibilities must be a

148

concomitant of states' rights, nor did the party's platform offer one specific proposal for change from within. Its formulators seemed to believe that American political and economic history had ended with Grover Cleveland.

They had not heard the voices of the jobless Louisianian as he snatched at the work slip in my Louisiana newspaper office, and the sweating charlatan who rose above himself at the bier of Huey Long. They could not comprehend the disillusion of a magnificent old Negro who believed that his Mississippi white people would do the right thing. They remained traditionalists, as was the kinsman who voted in spite of himself for Al Smith. They shut their eyes to the sorry significance of a Bilbo, pouring it on for the support of the hating and fearing.

It is a deafness and a blindness which must not persist, for there are other voices in the land.

12.

It's an Ideal Location

As EDITOR and publisher of the *Delta Democrat-Times* (circulation 13,000, rates on request), I have often been astonished and gratified by my fellow citizens' tolerant acceptance of editorial opinions which are contrary to theirs and of stories which many would prefer to go unpublished. At no greater cost than occasional nervousness, I have been able to denounce flaccid sheriffs, sundry community inequalities, drinking at football games, the city council, bonuses for veterans, and even the New Look, with the certainty that occasional subscription cancellations will be offset by new subscribers and that those who differ will be content to denounce me in turn.

But there is one sacrosanct topic which, even were I so minded—and I hastily add that I am not—I would not dare to discuss save in the most favorable terms. That topic is the advantages which Greenville, Mississippi, offers the prospective industrialist.

Were I to intimate, even indirectly, that our transportation facilities were not the most adequate, our tax structure not the most favorable, our raw materials not the most plentiful, our city government not the

150

most receptive and co-operative, and our labor supply not the most tractable, I would at that instant
become a civic pariah. Besides, they are.

At least once a month, and preferably more often,
a group known as our business leaders is summoned to
play collective host to Northern industrialists in search
of plant sites. In this welcoming assembly are, invariably, the mayor, all three bank presidents, the
managers of our two principal industries—both operated by Northern corporations—the district manager of the power company, the secretary of the
Chamber of Commerce, the executives of the principal retail stores, the city engineer, and, for occupational reasons, myself. Each has a role to play, and an
honest, hopeful one, as an authority on some phase of
the community: its housing and recreational and utility facilities, its industrial program, its tax rates, its
available labor, its collective attitude toward new
industry. And each visiting delegation gets our earnest,
whole-spirited attention.

If these industrial site-seekers can spare us as much
as a day of their time, they get to know a great deal
about Greenville. They see our wide, tree-blessed ave-
nues and older residential districts, the store fronts
of our business district, and the new suburban addi-
tions which prove our proud claim that our population has nearly doubled in twelve years. They are
dined and unlawfully wined in our country club or
in the pleasant hotel whose modernity surprises them.
Their brief cases are crammed with statistics and the

151

Chamber of Commerce's illustrated brochure; and even though they undoubtedly knew of it in advance, they are reminded of Mississippi's now successful experiment in industrial subsidization, the BAWI plan, the initials of which indicate its objective: Balance Agriculture with Industry.

After they have departed, we hold depressed post-mortems or more hopeful reviews of these conferences. Was the question about schools sufficiently answered by the figures on the new school bond issue? Was it clear that the supply of natural gas is as great as in any area in the valley? Did someone remember to give them the data on mean rainfall and humidity, and why in hell does it always have to rain when these fellows show up? What about emphasizing more strongly the poll that shows there are 2,700 men and women within a ten-mile radius who would welcome industrial employment?

Sometimes we sink into recriminations. Why in the name of all that is holy did Willis have to bring up the long-ago strike that was settled, anyhow, almost as soon as it began? Why does Lovell tell that anecdote about the three cows in the 1927 flood every time he gets a couple of drinks in him? Unless those men realize that the flood-control program has ended any flood threat, that foul story itself was enough to scare them off. And why talk so enviously of Natchez? It is just a matter of a few lucky breaks down there.

But even though Lovell's and Willis' mistakes may have cost us this particular $500,000 pay roll—it probably would not have been that much anyway—we go home with the optimistic knowledge that in another week or so the representatives of one of the largest buttonhole companies in the world will be with us. After all, what do Jackson and Meridian and Vicksburg have that we do not have, and look what we have besides. And even if this next outfit does not locate in Greenville, it is definite that it will settle someplace in Mississippi, and, boy, that is something.

It is one thing to laugh at these recurrent events, as we sometimes do among ourselves, but it is another thing to laugh them off. A Sinclair Lewis might find in them a newer *Main Street* theme; but in all truth, there is nothing shallow or humorous in the eventful current itself.

These monthly meetings are evidence of a tremendous competitive struggle, composed of many intersectional and intrasectional contests. On the outer fringes of the campaign for a more balanced and richer economy, towns within each Southern state are battling each other, but these are diversionary skirmishes, meaningful only in that the well-being of a Greenville may or may not come to surpass that of its sister Mississippi communities. More decisive is the competition among the Southern states for the decentralizing or expanding industries of the East and Midwest, for upon its outcome depends the relative development of entire states. But the elemental conflict is that which is being waged among the sepa-

153

rate regions of the nation for the industrial pay roll.

Thus it is that we in Greenville are happy over a Mississippi victory if a hill town in eastern Mississippi gets the factory for which we had fought, even though we find it hard to forgive the town's spokesmen for their base calumny that the Delta is fever ridden, populated only by lazy, rich planters, and inundated twice a year by the Mississippi. We are delighted even to learn that a paper mill is being built in Alabama, a viscose plant in Georgia, and a great, new chemical factory in Louisiana. For these accomplishments mean that we, the inclusive Southern we, are beginning to catch up after the long, lean, thoughtless years.

But, although the South is gaining ground in this intersectional, industrial war, it is not yet effecting thereby the basic decentralization of financial-industrial direction itself. The legacy of economic domination from outside still influences greatly not only our industrial development but our social and political thinking, so that it remains difficult for too many of us to distinguish between our own best long-range interests and the frequently conflicting best interests of our hereditary liege lords.

During my boyhood, that part of Louisiana in which I lived, and much of adjoining south Mississippi, were scarred and gutted by the harvest of the sawmills. The countryside was pocked with ugly little sawmill villages which thrived unhealthily while the timber lasted, then languished in decay after the pine and cypress forests had been cut away. We had no local timber millionaires. What we furnished was the trees, the labor, and some of the supervisory personnel. The resident managers were Northerners. Most of the timber and all of the profits it brought went somewhere else.

But the lumber companies were unchallenged. They were welcomed for their pay rolls; their resident executives were privileged citizens, and the interests of the local bankers and attorneys and businessmen were identical with theirs. If the sawyers wanted more money, they found the leading citizens of the lumber towns allied almost solidly against them. When legal involvements, from injury claims to land controversies, occurred, the best lawyers represented the companies. Only a maverick few among the politicians spoke out against the domination of the timber interests in local affairs. And when the policy of reforestation was mercifully adopted, it was only because the operators themselves saw the light. Before that happened, almost the whole of south Mississippi was cut bare, its land exhausted, its people reduced to marginal living, and its leaders so aroused, belatedly, that—going to the opposite extreme—the state enacted legislation which, until it was repealed, made it all but impossible for a foreign corporation to operate in Mississippi.

So, too, with the mineral resources, the transportation system, the few processing industries, and even the raw agricultural materials of the South. No more than twenty years ago it could be proved that, in its relationship to the East, the South was one great company town. This is less true today. Yet even now, control of most of the oil companies, the textile mills, the railroads, the steel mills, the utilities, and the major industrial plant lies in distant hands.

We are told that we made our bed and must lie in it; that the South chose more than a century ago to be and to remain agricultural and that we are just waking up. But it is not Southern decision which today preserves the old colonial status, but the consolidation of industrial-financial control in the East.

The techniques of control are multifold. Patent monopolies and freight-rate differentials. Protective manufacturing tariffs. The centralization of capital in the Eastern money markets resulting from a century of concentrated industrial development and the channeling of profits on the raw materials of the South and West. Political mastery. And willing Southern mercenaries.

Just as multiple are the results. In the New England and north central states are concentrated 89 per cent of the high-wage, skilled-worker, mobile industries—chemical processing, air conditioning, ceramics, electrical devices, scientific instruments, internal-combustion engines, radio equipment, plastic products, textile processing. In the East are located the life-insurance companies doing 95 per cent of the total volume. As of 1940—and the picture cannot have changed greatly since then—the total assets of each of at least fourteen Eastern corporations were larger than the assessed valuations of any of the Southern states. Five were life-insurance companies, the principal private financiers of enterprise. Four were banks, with chains of control extending down to the bankers of Greenville. Three were railroads, so adamant against the ending of freight-rate differentials. The others were the Standard Oil, United States Steel, General Motors, Alleghany Corporation, and Commonwealth and Southern, and for each of them the South represented principally a source of raw materials, a sales territory, or an area for branch operations.

And 2 per cent of the total number of American manufacturers, most of them based in the East and the Midwest, employed, as of 1944, 62 per cent of the total number of industrial workers. Sometimes their hearts bleed for their fellow men, too, as when a governor of Connecticut urged New England manufacturers to contribute $500,000 to aid in the unionization of Southern labor—in order to arrest the "drain of Northern industry into the sweatshop areas of the South."

Concede even that the North earned this monopoly because of superior initiative, thrift, know-how, determination, wisdom of choice, and a more skilled and intelligent population. The copybook virtues can be very real, and I have no wish to detract from the success stories so abundant in the history of New England, Pennsylvania, New York, and New Jersey. Let us admit, too, that branch plants in Mississippi are far better than no plants at all, and that these new industrial pay rolls have helped to increase our per capita income to two thirds of the national average even though the industrial profits have been skimmed off for consumption elsewhere. I am in complete accord with my fellow Greenvillians in trying to induce industries to locate in our city, even if their owners live in Tibet. A Northerner with new ideas may get a quick brushoff or worse, but a Northerner with a new factory—right this way, gentlemen, and do you realize the advantages of river transportation?

But why endorse that self-immolating Southern philosophy which identifies the objectives of the absentee owner with our own, and which provides Southern spokesmen for Eastern self-interest? Nonunion labor and wage-scale differentials are desirable to the industrialist in search of a branch-plant location, for example; and it is understandable that private utility companies would like to hamstring the Tennessee Valley Authority. It is not understandable that there should be such wide Southern support for these attitudes.

Of course, it is not majority support. But the South is not yet a place where the majority exercises economic or even political self-determination. The politico-economic alignments, especially in the towns and smaller cities of the South, are made through the traditional coalition of the banker, the lawyer representing absentee corporation interests, the large landowner, and the executive of existing local or branch industry. Flanking these leaders are an army of subordinates, the merchants, the professional men, usually the politicians, and more often than not the newspaper publisher.

This coalition is conservative not only by occupations and tradition but through social identification with the managerial and absent-owner groups. The spindle operator down at the mill may be dividing his pay check among them, but he is not sitting around in the locker room or the home bar, disinterring the remains of that damn radical who wrecked the country and discussing the alliance of Joe Stalin and Philip Murray.

When the late Grand Dragon Sam Green of the Ku Klux Klan explained from the depths of his Atlanta Klavern that he was not opposed to organized labor but that "the Klan is against Communism and unions are Communistic" he was seeking the support of this Southern coalition and trying to make the Klan respectable. But it is not actually the fear of Red rebellion that causes such Southern representatives of Northern industry and the industry hunters of the South to shrink from the ballooning specter of unionization. Rather, they are fearful that increased operating costs will reduce profits and jeopardize the already established industry, or that the prospective industry will shy away.

159

This point of view is not necessarily malicious. Once there was reason for the South to emphasize cheapness of labor as its principal attraction for industry. Low standards of literacy and health, an unskilled population, transportation handicaps, an individualistic, rural society's mistrust of collective effort—all these combined to make cheap labor the principal lure. And even today there is a hard practicality behind Southern emphasis of the willingness, the abundance, and the good behavior—the 100 per cent Americanism—of Southern workers. The intensity of the labor-management struggle elsewhere in industrial America must make the South seem like heaven to a strike-harassed manufacturer, even though that heaven is only temporary.

That is why we never mention our long-ago strike in Greenville, and why I should feel like a Judas when my newspaper reports that the CIO is seeking an election at the mill. Such stories may be upsetting to the next delegation from Toledo. We need the pay rolls. A dollar-an-hour minimum would be nice, but even fifty cents an hour, multiplied by 500 workers whom mechanization is shunting from the plantations, would add much to the local economy. And so our handful of dissenting Machiavellians do not protest too loudly. After all, if we get them here on a fifty-cent premise, the CIO and the AFL will come along soon.

Why becloud the issue by observing that in the organized textile mills of the South the average minimum wage has risen from 35 cents to 75 cents an hour, and that if in the wood-products industries alone the wages of white and Negro workers could be equalized, the spendable income of the South would increase a billion dollars a year? Let us get the new industry now and the less said the better.

This is part of a war for survival and for growth. As such, it is understandable. The coalition prospers and the town itself becomes more stable, even though the steady job at the new plant may be disillusioning to the new, fumbling employee from the farm.

But this alliance with distant interests cannot be condoned when it is formed in opposition to the TVA, which I am singling out as the paramount example both of regional development and of absentee recruiting of mercenary or thoughtless opposition. No part of the country stands to profit as much as does the South from the restitution and development of its resources and the increased purchasing power of its people. In the Tennessee Valley, the per capita income has risen in fifteen years from 40 to 70 per cent of the national average; land long ago abandoned has been made again fruitful through TVA-directed farming practices; new industries have come in, shutting their eyes to socialism where it profits them; and the Tennessee River, navigable now to Knoxville, is virtually flood-free. But I wish I had a dollar for every time I have heard my fellow citizens tell me that the TVA is Communistic and that we do not want any part of it.

And there is the pitifully special concern which we

161

show for the faraway manipulators of our economic destiny. No one in Greenville worried when my printers organized or when the unions invaded the locally owned machine works or cottonseed-oil mills. We are home folks, and we are not going to leave. When my employees first engaged in collective bargaining three years ago—and by coincidence, added a good many thousands of dollars to the annual pay roll— I wrote an editorial pointing out that Greenville now had a new $100,000 pay roll and that we certainly were entitled to a five-year tax exemption and a modern plant, to be built by a municipal bond issue and amortized over thirty years. Everyone laughed and said that we were lucky to have such a sense of humor. But the absentee owner is a disembodied ogre. No one smiles when the report gets out that Mr. Sewell Avery is upset in faraway Chicago because the mill organizers have come to town. My God, they may close down the mill just to show the union what they think of it.

The South, so proud in all things else, is in this respect prideless. Here is the unwholesome legacy of the colonial vassal, and it is as needless as it is abject. We have set too small store by the worth of human sweat, put too low a price upon what we have. Nowhere else in the United States is there such a happy conjunction of climate, end products, potential water power, diversity of resources, and hopeful determination to catch up with the rest of the country. Nowhere else is there such disparity from the norm, so many who lack so much. Nowhere else are sons and daughters the principal export commodity, not only because jobs are fewer but because the pay for the obtainable job is less.

The conviction that the South's economy rests on cheapness of labor antedates our late surge toward industrialization. Cotton was historically a product of unskilled labor and had to be produced cheaply to compete in the markets of the world. Cotton was the South's one cash commodity. Thus the unskilled field hand, slave and free, set the South's wage standards, depressing inevitably the incomes of all who rode on his back. And all did.

When I was a boy, the farmers used to say that no Negro was worth more than a dollar a day. They do not say it as often now. But the insistence that the Southern worker, white and Negro, should be grateful for less than his fellows elsewhere, persists; and boasting that his costs of living are lower, we forget that his standards of living are lower yet.

It is time that we remember this disparity; time to recognize more positive heritages. We have too long undervalued our manpower, wasted our resources, and gone hat in hand for the capital to put us on our feet. We have more to offer the cruising industrialist than docility, cheapness, and a blank check.

For instance, take Greenville, Mississippi. . . .

13.

The Deeper Wound

THE ACCUSATION that the white South discriminates severely against the Negro cannot be dis-
proved. *To discriminate* means variously to discern
differences, to note or set apart as different, and to
deal with unequally. Each definition fits. Discerning
differences in physical appearance and in superficial
behavior between the white man and the Negro, we
have for three centuries set the Negro apart, linked
his behavior—particularly his unfavorable behavior
—with his color and antecedents, and proceeded to
treat him with manifest unfairness.

Most Southerners prefer not to talk about discrimination. When we do, we usually speak defensively
and with considerable truth of the mistreatment of
Jews, Indians, Mexican and Oriental Americans, and
the yet unassimilated immigrant. We say that intoler-
ance bestrides the nation and the world and that its
menace is dangerously minimized when the accusation is limited to the South's manifestations alone.

Some of us also seek to explain that man's ancient
and irrational antipathies for the dissimilar in culture,
in religion, and even in nationality have been aggra-

164

vated in the South by the peculiar relationship between the white man and the Negro.

That relationship has been abnormal and disquieting in almost every aspect. For the first two hundred
years of his residence in America, the Negro was property, comprising at slavery's end two thirds of the
South's wealth; and that wealth, together with much
of the rest of the South's assets, was wiped out by war
and without compensation. The emancipated Negro
became a symbol of the conquered South and its political subordination, through his freedom itself and because of his relatively brief period of political co-domi-
nance during the Reconstruction years; and since the
Negro remained in the South after the political manipulators of Reconstruction had departed, Southern antagonism was transferred to the ignorant and generally innocent masses who had responded to the
carpetbagger and scalawag. Reconstruction's very
small number of beneficial results—notably the impetus to the public-school systems of the South—were
forgotten. The very real excesses, the violence, the
looting, and the political humiliation were remembered and sometimes exaggerated in memory; and the
Negro was held to blame. In the dismal aftermath of
war and throughout the long, still incomplete economic rehabilitation and reorientation of the cotton
South, the Negro became, for hapless men no better
off than he, a hateful symbol of dog-eat-dog competition, and for the landowner and employer a source of
labor the value of which was measured almost solely

in terms of its enforced cheapness, docility, and lack of skill. And ever since Emancipation, the Negro has represented to the past-conditioned white majority a political and social threat which must be kept dormant. Against such a background, it is difficult to give credence to the frequent protestations that in the South the white man and the Negro understand each other, that their life together would be idyllic if they were let alone, and that they have a great affection for each other. Except for a relatively small number of individual relationships, mostly in the master-servant category or in the rarer sphere of intellectual recognition, the white man demonstrates little affection or respect for the Negro. And certainly the Negro's attitude must be a corollary to the white man's attitude. It is improbable that the Negro loves a people who once held him in slavery, whose concessions to his citizenship have been grudging and slow, and who have made his predicated inferiority the primary unifying factor in their political, social, and economic behavior.

Instead, the two groups go their separate ways, as far as separateness can be maintained, in common mistrust; and throughout this strangely communal life that is lived together yet apart are woven the multiple threads of discrimination.

I do not intend to catalogue the unfair dealings or to underline their frustrating effect upon the nine million Negroes of the South. They are so apparent and have been so unceasingly presented that no reminders are necessary. Neither shall I expand upon the encouraging fact that discrimination is diminishing in direction, scope, and intensity throughout the South, partly because of national pressures and the new militancy of the Negro and partly because of an awakening Southern conscience. Let us consider instead another phase of discrimination which is too often overlooked: the woeful effect upon the white South of the heritage of unfair dealing with a minority people. We are properly concerned with what the white man in the South and elsewhere has done to the Negro; but we should be likewise concerned with the spiritually and materially corrosive effect that the Negro, by his presence on such inflexibly prescribed terms of inferiority, has had upon the conscience and the welfare of the white South.

In the spring of 1949, a small group of white and Negro citizens met in our town, at the request of the Negroes, to discuss discrimination in law enforcement. The complaint was not the expected one. Instead, these Negro ministers, teachers, and businessmen asked for more drastic punishment for Negro lawbreakers. They had been aroused by a series of murders, assaults, and robberies committed by Negroes against Negroes and by the casualness with which the white population accepted such crimes.

As I listened to their bill of particulars I felt guilty myself. My newspaper, in common with every other newspaper in the South, had given little space to stories of Negro wrongdoing. A Negro knife fight merited only a sentence or two, a Negro slaying a few paragraphs. The trials of Negroes who killed other Negroes were briefly reported. Only once had I commented editorially that the punishment for such major crimes was far lighter than would have been the case had the principals been white or had the victim of a Negro offender been white. Actually, most of the sentences were less severe than in the rarer cases in which white defendants were found guilty of offenses against Negroes.

All of us at that meeting knew that in all-Negro cases the prosecution and defense attorneys traded readily so as not to clutter up the dockets with long and expensive trials, and that it was not unusual for planters and other employers of "good" Negroes to beg off their favored or direly needed tenants and employees when they ran afoul of the law, or to arrange extralegal paroles, especially during cotton-chopping and cotton-picking time. All my life I had heard and repeated jocose stories of Negro crap-game and bedroom killings and lesser fracases as if they were remote from suffering and death and the orderly intent of society. And not infrequently I had listened to a Negro Saturday-night badman, summoned by an indulgent boss, regaling the white folks with lurid accounts of how he mowed down an adversary with a Police Positive or trimmed him to size with a piece of two-by-four, a razor, or the spring-bladed knife that is known affectionately as a crab-apple switch.

It is undoubtedly true that white tolerance of Negro

168

wrongdoing is at least equaled by the uneducated, low-income Negro's uncritical reacceptance of the killer and lesser lawbreaker whom society has released after inadequate punishment or no punishment at all. Among the Negro masses there is no ostracism of the freed murderer and thief; and in most criminal cases involving Negroes, it is extremely difficult to find witnesses willing to testify in behalf of the law. I think that these attitudes result in part from fear that after the defendant is freed, or serves a short term, he will take revenge, and in part from a tacit conspiracy against the law itself, since the Negro has no part in the law's administration. And certainly this indifference is encouraged by the philosophical conclusion that if such goings-on don't bother the white people why should they bother the Negroes.

The grave Negroes who asked for more severe punishment for criminal members of their race had a sympathetic audience. They were assured that the judges, the county and district attorney, the sheriff, and the chief of police would be informed of their request and urged to accede as far as they were able. Our newspaper gave a full account of the meeting, and I wrote several editorials in support of even-handed justice. But it is doubtful that anything more than that will be done for a long time. The South's judges, juries, and law officers are almost as warped as are the rest of us by the acceptance of Negro lawlessness—where only Negroes are involved—as inevitable, of no great importance, and often even amusing. The great majority of crimes of violence in the South are committed by Negroes against Negroes. The Negro also commits more crimes of violence against the white man than the white man commits against Negroes; and the white man commits more crimes of violence against other white men than against Negroes. There is a different kind of justice for each category, and under this twisted application of the law the lasting victim is law itself. Because we discriminate against the Negro in its application, we find it all but impossible to discriminate between abstract right and wrong.

"You keep yourself out of the burying ground," the employer tells his erring Negro employee, "and I'll keep you out of jail."

There are other abstractions which are likewise warped. During my boyhood, our family cook for several years—until she left town with a free-spending logging-camp hand—was a lusty young Negro woman whose behavior was as uninhibited away from her work as it was decorous in the kitchen. Daisy's weakness was men, plenty of men. She had two illegitimate children. During the six or seven years she cooked for us she lived with four different men whom she impartially called her husbands. Ever so often Daisy was temporarily incapacitated because of fights with one of her paramours or with a jealous woman, and once she was shot in the hip and painfully wounded by a disappointed suitor. When she returned from the hospital she was a family heroine and we children regretted only that the location of her wound prevented her showing it to us. Daisy was a bigamist, an adulteress, and a high-stepper, and we all knew it; and we enjoyed her state of sinfulness far more than we did her brief periods of salvation following a revival or an unhappy love affair.

Daisy was not unique among the cooks and maids and gardeners and tenants who worked for us and for our friends, nor was our family's acceptance of her unusual. We would not have tolerated such immorality in a white employee; had I ever attempted to discuss within the family circle the affairs of any of the town's amiable white strumpets I would have been sent from the room and punished, for I was not even supposed to know about them. But we all laughed about Daisy, and since the only Negroes we knew were servants and laborers, we surmised that their free and easy mating was natural and inescapable and common to all Negroes.

Where two standards of morality exist side by side, it is inconceivable that the baser cannot affect the higher standard. Again it is the abstracts of right and wrong that become clouded and their application made difficult. In subtle ways, and in ways not so subtle, the discrimination reacts against the discriminator, so that a confused amorality supplants moral force and the light-skinned child is taken for granted along with the darker, easy mother.

It may be argued that such blights are largely intangible, and that the sexual laxity of the Negro can have no lasting ill-effect upon the condoning white majority. That may be, though I doubt it. But there are other and less remote results of discriminatory dealing. The worst of these is the tolerance of individual or group dishonesty when it is practiced only against the Negro.

I am told, and I believe, that there is far less stealing from Negro tenants and employees by white landowners and employers than there was a generation ago. Various reasons are given; the times are better, the Negroes are smarter now, the ability and the integrity of the employer have improved. There is no way to determine how widespread this kind of dishonesty was in the past nor how general it is now; the extent is less significant than the manner in which it is accepted. A farmer or a businessman can be a known thief in his dealings with Negroes and not lose caste among his honest fellows to any appreciable degree. True enough, they may be critical or contemptuous behind his back, and when he dies they may recall unfavorable and unprinted anecdotes about him; but, albeit he is a common thief, he can borrow money at the bank, get elected to local office, and mingle socially with incorrupt men without challenge.

The excuse that is offered in behalf of the dishonest farmer has become a part of Southern folklore. The tenant, it is said, steals all year round from the landowner, but the landowner steals only once a year at settlement time. The temptation on each side is great, especially in the marginal operations that are characteristic of so much of the South's agricultural enterprises. The cheap, unskilled Negro farm laborer is in reality the most expensive labor of all; shirking, carelessness, pilfering, and ignorance undoubtedly take a toll from the Southern employer far greater than the reciprocal subtraction of unscrupulous management. And it would be unfair, moreover, to label employee-cheating as a Southern phenomenon. Everywhere the weak and the ignorant tempt the unscrupulous and strong, especially in those places and at such times that economic survival is difficult. But the South still discriminates between the conscienceless man whose victim is a Negro and the conscienceless man whose victim is a white. That is the grievous difference to which an unhealthy past has inured us.

Nor is Southern acceptance of dishonesty toward the Negro restricted to the employer-employee relationship. There is scarcely a political subdivision in the South—state, county, town, or ward—in which the Negro is not treated unfairly as a citizen. The most flagrant example is the disbursement of school moneys. The constitution of every Southern state proclaims that the school systems for the two races shall be separate but equal. That equality is a myth—in physical plants, in pay, in transportation, in curriculums, and in teaching standards. Everyone knows it. Almost everyone agrees that something should be done about it. But the pocketbook deflects the appeal to the conscience; and, to our shame, Federal court action is supplying the impetus.

And so with every community facility from recreational areas to streets and hospitals, and the most shocking aspect is not that the Negro receives so much less but that the white South is yet only mildly disturbed by the discrepancies. We still protest only faintly the fact that the Negro gets less than is his due because for three hundred years we have looked upon him as a subhuman inferior who is not to be included in our ideal of equal justice. And if the Negro is harmed thereby, we are harmed tenfold.

There are material damages that are easier to comprehend than the dangers of moral anesthesia. Indifference to the Negro's health—the assumption that his illnesses have no relationship to our own—has maimed our bodies together with his, for no one has ever devised a color barrier that bacilli will respect. Early in 1949, the Mississippi State Board of Health sent a mobile blood-testing unit to our county to ascertain the incidence of syphilis. Dr. Felix Underwood, director of the Board of Health, has awakened Mississippi in recent years to the importance of public health, and his department is an outstanding one; but the blood tests in our county and elsewhere gave evidence of the distance yet to be traveled. The tests indicated that nearly 25 per cent of the county's Negro population was infected with syphilis:—one in four of the people who, in the structure of Southern society, perform personal services of every kind—cooking the food, nursing the children, and laundering the clothes. If the tests had shown as high an infection rate among the white population, we would have been panic-swept. But Negroes? Oh, that's different. They always have had venereal disease—or tuberculosis, or typhoid fever—because they're Negroes.

As with health, so with living standards in general. We do not notice the Negro slum because it is as much a part of our landscape as is the cotton field. We attribute the Negro's lack of technical and craft skills to a racial inability to learn. We insist that a day's work by a Negro is not worth that same day's work performed by a white man. The result is a reduction in the white man's earning potential and the over-all income of a region whose professional men, businessmen, and craftsmen wonder why their efforts do not produce the incomes earned elsewhere through no greater effort.

The material loss is great. The spiritual destruction is far greater, for discrimination has infected the white South with a moral sickness. We are plagued and dwarfed by the mental reservations which still accompany our endorsement of the Christian ethic, the democratic concept of justice, and the economic principle of full human usefulness; intentionally or unconsciously we exclude from their application almost one third of our population. And though that one third has suffered grievously as a result, the soul of the white South has suffered a deeper wound.

14.

Out of Inquietude

IF THE SOUTH had ever agreed with the rest of the nation that it is primarily a collection of unfavorable statistics, it would have lost long ago the self-esteem which is an essential requisite for cultural survival. But the price of ignoring the statistics is their certain perpetuation.

For a hundred years the statistics have been inexorably produced by invasion and political obliteration, by bankruptcy and a debilitating agricultural economy, by uninspired leadership and a spiritually destructive human relationship. The legacy they represent in sum total is one that has impoverished rather than enriched. It has been balanced in part by a stubborn, defensive pride and a regional devotion as baffling to the observer as they are nourishing to the Southerner himself. Love of region and self-esteem have been the South's emotional antidotes to otherwise inescapable degeneration.

As antidotes they have served their purpose admirably. As substitutes for reality they have been insufficient. The statistics remain. And the South of a mature purposefulness need ignore them no longer in fear that material fact may destroy spiritual certainty.

In the eleven states of the Southeast live some 35 million people, a smaller proportion of the nation's population than they represented fifty years ago. The out-migration quickens. During the war years, the South lost one million more inhabitants than it gained. Of its young men who served in the armed forces, one in seven found greener pastures elsewhere after demobilization. Of its young men who remained at home, proportionately more were rejected for physical and mental disabilities than in any other region of the nation.

The states which the one in seven forsook receive only 10 per cent of the nation's industrial wages, although they contain one fifth of the population. The average per capita income of their citizens has more than doubled in twenty years, to $883, but it is only 67 per cent of the national average. It is understandable that the young men are still restless, still intent on the distant field. Their migration has left in the South's labor force far more adolescents and old men than are present in the nation's labor force as a whole. And those who leave and those who remain at home are alike handicapped in their work, for only one third of the South's population has been educated beyond the eighth grade. In this day of the machine, one Southerner in four has less than a fifth-grade education. The principal migration is from the farms of the South. Of the 160 million acres of American farm land which erosion has reduced to inutility, nearly 100 mil-

177

lion, more than 60 per cent of the total, lie in the South. On the useful and useless land, two thirds of all Southern farmers try to make their livings by growing cotton and tobacco.

Two years out of three, the Southern farmer produces far more cotton than is consumed. Although he prides himself on his individualism and is suspicious of his distant government, the cotton farmer is solvent only because of Federal agricultural benefits. And the Federal government provides, principally through payments to farmers, 22 per cent of the South's total income.

Overproducing its field crops, the South does not yet produce sufficient dairy products, meat, poultry, eggs, vegetables, and feedstuffs to care for its own needs.

Nor is this agricultural instability balanced by industrial productivity. In the entire United States, 36 billion dollars in wages and salaries were paid in 1946, but the South's share was only a little more than 3½ billion. The average annual wages of the Southern industrial worker rose from $1,019 in 1939 to $1,798 in 1944, a greater increase percentagewise than for the nation as a whole; but the national average wage was $2,302. Although the South's rate of industrial growth surpassed the rest of the nation's during and since the war, industrial diversification is still distant. Textiles, wood products, food products, and chemicals account for nearly two thirds of the South's industrial output, with textiles making up nearly one third of

178

the total. The South does not yet have industrial capital and management and a trained labor supply. It lacks the great life-insurance companies and investment banks necessary to provide capital investment. It is still primarily an exporter of raw products for processing elsewhere rather than a processor itself.

Against this background of agricultural and industrial lags, other unfavorable statistics are inevitable. The South has the fewest doctors and the fewest hospital beds for each thousand of its population. Its venereal disease, tuberculosis, and infant and maternal mortality rates are the nation's largest. Its expenditures upon its educable children are the smallest and its illiteracy rate the highest. Less than 5 per cent of its rural homes have baths. Its people commit proportionately the greatest number of crimes of violence and escape with the least degree of punishment. They cast the smallest vote in relation to their numbers. And so on, throughout a somber catalogue.

All of this is well enough known. What is less well known is that, except in population loss, the South is moving upward on every gauge by which the progress of a civilization can be measured. Ours is no longer a problem of direction but of acceleration.

More land is being restored in the South through terracing, crop rotation, and pasturing than anywhere else in the nation. Manufacturing income has almost tripled in ten years. In every Southern state, new hospitals are being built, state health departments expanded, disease reduced, school systems extended.

179

The giant turbines of the Tennessee Valley Authority put water to work for man. The white-faced Herefords graze where once the mined earth cried out for rest. Around the multiplying factories are lined the automobiles of workers from the gutted hills and the once-listless towns. The young saplings rise by plan from the land where the forests were planlessly slain. Everywhere the change is sure.

There is a material and a moral urgency to this Southern metamorphosis. Ours is a region surpassingly endowed and as wastefully negligent of its endowment. No other region has as generous a combination of equable climate, productive soil in spite of abuse, actual and potential hydroelectric power, timber and mineral reserves, and human resources. No other region has made as little productive use of what it embraces. No other region has destroyed so much of itself.

If the 35 million Southerners were to attain a standard of living equal to that enjoyed by the rest of the nation, their material demands would add 15 billion dollars in needed goods and services to the nation's consumption totals. Could they divest themselves of the searing heritages of mistrust and fear, they would subtract immeasurably from the bill of particulars by which the enemies of democracy seek to negate its meaning throughout the world. These are the South's twin mandates to itself. They cannot be carried out through the force-feeding of new practices and ideals.

180

The realization of their urgency must come from within.

The statistics cannot be evaded. It is useless for Southerners to pretend that the region we love is not identical with the region whose faults and needs have been so thoroughly tabulated. But the statistics can be changed. They were created out of the Southern past and the past does not endure even when men insist that it is unending. The Southern legacies are not eternal and need not be accepted when reason suggests their rejection; but before rejection or retention, they must be inspected and evaluated and their sources understood.

So it is that the South must look behind even as it moves ahead, recognizing the fetters of an agrarian tradition which could have been altogether wholesome, but which was degraded through a one-crop economy, the enslavement of man, and the pitiable makeshift of tenancy on land that men had ruined and were in turn ruined by. The agrarian past must be honestly weighed. Against the manors it reared and the virtues it possessed must be balanced the flight of intellect which it impelled, the prejudices it inspired, the political miasma in which it was shrouded, and the quantitative limitations of the distinctive culture it produced. And we must recognize, too, its peculiar contribution to the American dilemma arising from the presence of the Negro, the abused, retarded, identifiable stranger of 300 years whose similarity of aspirations and dissimilarity of race have created in the

181

white South a unity of resistance which is the principal cohesive element in its regional solidarity.

I have spent a good many hours, nor altogether fruitfully, reading or listening to proposals for solving the South's problems. Some of them were convincing, some unrealistic, some downright absurd. Their principal point of agreement is that the Southern predicament has been primarily economic, a conclusion which requires no great wisdom to reach.

To these earnest blueprints I have nothing to contribute save a certainty that the mandatory first step today is to make the availability and the quality of public education in the South at least comparable to prevailing national standards, so that our man power may acquire equal productive capacities in the crafts and arts and sciences, and the wider social vision that is education's first obligation to society. But as this equal proficiency is attained it must concurrently find agricultural, industrial, and professional usefulness in the South, else the migration of the young and the talented will increase as skills are acquired which cannot be employed at home. The goal of agricultural-industrial balance must be set beside the goal of education. There is nothing profound in such observations. They have been made many times before, but as long as the goals are unachieved there is need for repetition.

Yet even the absolute attainment of economic objectives would not in itself resolve the racial dilemma that

182

is not restricted to the South but aggravated here because of the numbers involved and attitudes generated by law and folkways for three centuries. Education, greater economic security, and protective legislation can soften the impact of racial antipathies, but there is no formula for ending them except the formula which man discovers within himself.

The best that can be expected in the ascertainable future from the South's attainment of national levels in income and education is a more rapid amelioration of the discriminatory aspects of the white-Negro relationship. The harshest manifestations of prejudice exist where the living standards of the dominant and the submerged groups are alike low, and where the numerical pressures of the submerged and dissimilar are interpreted by the dominant as constituting a political, economic, or social threat to the established controls. Since the living standards are being raised and the numerical pressures reduced throughout the South, greater and rapid amelioration appears certain.

Through migration, the Negro population in the South is decreasing in relation to the white population, so that in no Southern state and in less than 180 counties is the Negro in a majority. Until now this migration has been principally voluntary and motivated by ambition or resentment or both, but it is being quickened involuntarily as the machine replaces the man and the mule.

The admission that the reduction of the ratio of Negro to white in the South will hasten the South's

183

over-all progress is also an admission of democratic failure; but as tragic as the implication is, the fact remains that if the Negro exodus continues, it will contribute at least as much to the South's economic transformation and to white acceptance of the Negro as a citizen as will any other presently foreseeable factor. The Negro vote, for example, is the least opposed in Virginia, North Carolina, and Tennessee, the states with the smallest Negro populations and the greatest industrial balance and agricultural diversification. Pigsty housing, inferior schooling, and inadequate medical facilities are the least condoned or accepted as inevitable in those areas of the South where the white majority is the largest.

But the South cannot wait for this bleak and negative impetus to development. Even if half of the nine million Southern Negroes were to leave, the remainder would constitute an unending reproach until they were recognized as citizens entitled to the same political rights and the same economic opportunity and capable of making equal contributions to democratic America.

Such recognition is the paramount necessity for the South today, and for all America. The integration of the Negro in our national life has an importance more immediately imperative than are domestic or even moral considerations. In the unresolved struggle between the democratic and the totalitarian concepts, the exclusion of the American Negro from full and uncontested participation in the democratic scheme pro-

184

vides the totalitarian protagonists with an effective weapon. The skin colors of three quarters of the world's population are black or brown or yellow. It is to this questioning, undecided majority that the Communist propagandist addresses his calculated disparagement of democracy as bearing a label "For Whites Only—All Others Keep Off."

I would like now to set aside the problems and the statistics and turn again to the legacy of regionalism. The Southerner does not love his country the less because of his self-identification with the comprehensible part of the whole. America is vast and many-sided, but a man's valley and hillside and state are near and intimate; and if there is any antidote to our mounting reliance upon distant, impersonal, and centralized power it is the regional attachment which, by virtue of long identification with his background, the Southerner possesses to a greater extent than do the rest of America's people.

I know that I am no better citizen than the immigrant's son, and it may be that I accept more lightly than he the privileges already won for us both; but I find serenity and sureness in the knowledge that to the river where we wait with guns for the mallard's winter flight my people came long ago with more purposeful weapons, some to prosper and some to lose what they found. Perhaps their small triumphs compensate for the later failures, perhaps their defeats remind us that there is nothing lost that cannot somehow be re-

185

gained. I cannot travel through the valley of Virginia nor along the Mississippi without experiencing a quickening of the blood; if my sons or even strangers are with me, my tongue loosens and I want to tell them of the people who settled and fought and clung there, for they were my people; and if the allegiance is sentimental it is not shallow. I understand the forces that fashioned these men. I am at home with their spirits.

This may be provincialism, but there is nothing unhealthy in it. The sense of intimate identification with a region fortifies the will to make it more nearly perfect and secure; and as the part is strengthened so is the whole. It is only when loyalty makes the regional patriot blind to imperfection and resentful of inspection that it becomes a deteriorative force; the obligation to examine, to protest and to propose change must accompany affection, else devotion can destroy. Too many Southerners fail to perceive this corollary; defiant and resentful of the alien critic, they are even more enraged by the native censor, stigmatizing him as a nest-fouler and suggesting that he should go elsewhere if he is not satisfied with what he finds.

I prefer to remain dissatisfied. I hope that there will never come a time when my sons or their sons will look about them and be content; for the soul is nurtured on inquietude: the soul of a man, the soul of a region, the soul of a nation. Out of inquietude the South, so long bemused in the twilight of its self-satisfaction, stirs now before the dawn.

186